DIALOGUE *of the* HEART

Father Martin McGee is a Benedictine monk and a chaplain in Worth Abbey School, Sussex. Originally from County Mayo, he studied arts at University College, Galway, before teaching French for more than a decade in County Louth. *Dialogue of the Heart* is his second book, following *Christian Martyrs for a Muslim People*, which tells the poignant story of the nineteen priests and sisters assassinated by Islamic fundamentalists in Algeria in the mid-1990s.

DIALOGUE
of the HEART

Christian–Muslim Stories of Encounter

Martin McGee, OSB

ORBIS BOOKS

Maryknoll, New York 10545

ORBIS BOOKS
Maryknoll, New York 10545

Fathers and Brothers
MARYKNOLL™

Founded in 1970, Orbis Books endeavors to publish works that enlighten the mind, nourish the spirit, and challenge the conscience. The publishing arm of the Maryknoll Fathers and Brothers, Orbis seeks to explore the global dimensions of the Christian faith and mission, to invite dialogue with diverse cultures and religious traditions, and to serve the cause of reconciliation and peace. The books published reflect the views of their authors and do not represent the official position of the Maryknoll Society. To learn more about Maryknoll and Orbis Books, please visit our website at www.maryknollsociety.org.

Library of Congress Cataloging-in-Publication Data

Names: McGee, Martin, author.
Title: Dialogue of the heart : Christian-Muslim stories of encounter / Martin McGee OSB.
Description: Maryknoll : Orbis Books, 2017. | Originally published: Dublin, Ireland : Veritas, 2015. | Includes bibliographical references.
Identifiers: LCCN 2017002832 (print) | LCCN 2017019897 (ebook) | ISBN 9781608337040 (e-book) | ISBN 9781626982390 (pbk.)
Subjects: LCSH: Islam—Relations—Christianity. | Christianity and other religions—Islam. | Monks—Algeria.
Classification: LCC BP172 (ebook) | LCC BP172 .M3934 2017 (print) | DDC 261.2/7—dc23
LC record available at https://lccn.loc.gov/2017002832

To Fr Jean-Pierre Schumacher OCSO
A True Follower of St Benedict
& Lover of the Muslim Soul

Table of Contents

INTRODUCTION: To Go Beyond Fear   9

Part 1 – The Monks of Tibhirine:
Men of Prayer alongside a People of Prayer

CHAPTER ONE: Pilgrims of Friendship: Notre-Dame
                  de L'Atlas, Morocco   19
CHAPTER TWO: Father Jean-Pierre: Happiness is
                  Found in Relationships   27
CHAPTER THREE: Brother Luc: The Impact of Sanctity   36
CHAPTER FOUR: Brother Michel: A Lover of the
                  Muslim Soul   43
CHAPTER FIVE: Father Christian: Discovering God's
                  Presence in Each Other   54

Part 2 – The Algerian Church: The Gift of Encounter

CHAPTER SIX: Learning to Love Our Muslim
                  Neighbours   77
CHAPTER SEVEN: Gospel Encounters   88
CHAPTER EIGHT: A Look of Admiration: Friendship, the
                  Core of Inter-religious Dialogue   95
CHAPTER NINE: Loving Those Who Are Different   101
CHAPTER TEN: Surprised by Love: The Heart of
                  Christian–Muslim Dialogue   108
CHAPTER ELEVEN: Pierre and Mohamed: No Greater Love 119
CHAPTER TWELVE: Love Hopes All Things: What Future
                  for Christian–Muslim Relations?   128

Appendices

APPENDIX ONE: Testament of Christian de Chergé   139
APPENDIX TWO: If the Other Were Really to Become
                 My Brother   141
APPENDIX THREE: A Doctrinal Note on How Christians
                 and Muslims Speak of God: The
                 French Bishops' Conference   149

ACKNOWLEDGEMENTS   155

INTRODUCTION
To Go Beyond Fear

Many people in the developed world and elsewhere are becoming more and more concerned about Islam. Recent years have seen many atrocities committed in the name of Islam, an Islam to which the vast majority of Muslims would not subscribe. The recent massacre (7 January 2015) by Islamic extremists of twelve people in the offices of the French satirical weekly *Charlie Hebdo,* and the subsequent killing two days later of four Jewish hostages, has spread fear and panic throughout the western world.

Then there are the reports of *Boko Haram* and ISIS atrocities that appear with chilling regularity in the media. In the face of all these horror stories, it would hardly be surprising if Christians and Muslims begin to retreat more and more into their respective social ghettoes and to look at each other with increasing suspicion. Such a reaction would, of course, only play into the hands of extremists on both sides and stoke the fires of violence. The challenge for Christians and Muslims is to build bridges of understanding and friendship and to reject the easy option of demonising each other.

Fear is contagious and, as St John tells us, the only antidote to fear is love. 'There is no fear in love, but perfect love casts out fear' (1 Jn 4:18). This book is about going beyond fear and daring to love. It tries to encourage people at grassroots level – parish clergy, pastoral workers, Church members and all people of goodwill – to see that they have a vital role to play in furthering Christian–Muslim dialogue by getting to know and love their Muslim neighbours. To embolden people to take the first step in reaching out, I draw on inspiring stories of Christian–Muslim encounters taken from the lives of the Tibhirine monks and the Church in North Africa. Stories, as Jesus shows us, are often more powerful than abstract ideas because they appeal to our hearts as well as to our heads. They make room for the Holy Spirit to challenge us to conversion and to action.

One person who resolutely reached out to Muslims was St John Paul II. He took to heart the teaching of *Nostra Aetate*, the Conciliar Declaration which threw open the doors of the Catholic Church to friendship and dialogue with people of other faiths. In writing this book I was struck by the fidelity of St John Paul II to the teaching of this document. In inviting the various faith communities to join him for the first World Day of Prayer for Peace in Assisi, Italy, on 27 October 1986 he showed a willingness to risk misunderstanding in the service of dialogue and fidelity to the teaching of the Council. And many people within the Roman Curia were taken aback by his gesture. Shortly afterwards he addressed the Curia and spelled out unambiguously his thinking on inter-religious dialogue. One can sense his passion for dialogue in the following quotation from this important address: 'There is *only one* divine plan for every single human being who comes into this world (cf. Jn 1:9), one single origin and goal, whatever may be the colour of his skin, the historical and geographical framework within which he happens to live and act, or the culture in which he grows up and expresses himself. The differences are a less important element when confronted with the unity which is radical, fundamental and decisive.'[1] The story of the

---

1. Pope John Paul II's Christmas Address to Roman Curia, 22 December 1986, www.ewtn.com/library

Tibhirine monks and of the North African Church in Algeria and Morocco celebrates this radical unity.

A DEEPER SHARING OF OUR COMMON HUMANITY

In the first half of this book I look at the lives of four of the Tibhirine monks, one of them still alive, to learn what they can teach us about relating to our Muslim neighbours. Many of you reading this book will have heard about the martyrdom of seven of the monks of Tibhirine in Algeria in 1996. Some of you will also have seen the film *Of Gods and Men* which sensitively portrays their decision to remain at Tibhirine and face the possibility of death in solidarity with their beleaguered Muslim neighbours. This film captured the imagination of many in the West, enabling Christians and others to envisage a deeper sharing of our common humanity, and faith in the one God, with our Muslim neighbours. The lives of the Tibhirine monks teach us that love is the most effective way of overcoming fear of the other.

Father Christian, one of the martyred Tibhirine monks, wrote in his Spiritual Testament: 'My death will of course prove right those who have dismissed me as naïve or idealistic: Let him tell us now what he thinks about it!'[2] Father Christian, unlike many of us, sought to remain faithful to the fullness of the Gospel teaching which challenges us to get to know and love our neighbours, whoever they may be. The monks of Tibhirine and the remnant of the Christian Church in Algeria and Morocco show us the cost of this high ideal but they also show us what can be achieved when we begin to live the Gospel more fully. As Fr Jean-Pierre, one of the two Tibhirine monks who escaped

---

2. See Appendix 1 for the full text of Fr Christian's Spiritual Testament. All translations from the French in this book are my own.

being kidnapped, remarks: 'The example of the brothers in their relationships with people, with Muslims, shows that one can become real brothers, in communion, together, in depth and not only on the surface. In depth before God. Certain people have lived this. It's not uncommon.'[3] The monks of Tibhirine demonstrated in their lives 'the good zeal' which St Benedict encouraged his monks to practise, namely, to seek first of all the good of our neighbour. And it is this good zeal that breaks down barriers of fear and distrust and discloses our common humanity, brothers and sisters of a common Father.

The Discovery of the Best in the Other

In May 2007 I attended a meeting of the European Coordinators of Monastic Inter-religious Dialogue (MID), which was hosted by the monks of Midelt.[4] Two presentations on dialogue in the Moroccan Church were given by Fr Jacques Levrat.[5] For twenty years Fr Jacques had directed a research library, *La Source*, which specialised in the cultural patrimony of Morocco. This library contained no Christian material. However, as a result of his living contact with the Muslim intellectual elite a dialogue of the heart ensued in which both sides were changed. For Fr Jacques, a dialogue is successful when both sides are victors, when both sides have been able to deepen their own religious identity. In this type of encounter people draw near to each other. 'Meeting the other challenges me, works upon me, changes me,' he said.

Father Jacques distinguishes dialogue from conversation and negotiation. In conversation we are limited by social

---

3. *Le Figaro Magazine*, 5 February 2011.
4. The surviving Tibhirine monks refounded the monastery of Notre-Dame de l'Atlas in Morocco, eventually settling at Midelt in the year 2000.
5. Father Levrat died on 6 February 2013.

conventions so there are things we don't say to each other. In negotiation we are involved in a political process where we look for a consensus or a practical solution to a problem; whereas dialogue always has as its objective the discovery of the other, the discovery of the best in the other. In every person there is a valet and a son of a king. We must address, said Fr Jacques, the son of the king in dialogue so that the son of the king will answer us. We must go beyond fear. Dialogue opens new pathways; it never comes to an end. The famous Fr Albert Peyriguère, who engaged in dialogue with Islam in Morocco before the Second Vatican Council, used to tell the story of his close relationship with the local imam. Their close relationship grew out of their common concern and work for the poor. One day the imam said to him: 'It won't be long now before we go to meet our Maker. We will hold hands and whichever of us is shown to be right and enters heaven first will drag along the other person with him!'

Dialogue Not Reserved for the Specialist

With Muslim migration to Europe and elsewhere, Christians are coming into more and more contact with Muslims. With increased contact people begin to get to know each other so prejudices and fears begin to melt away and, in many cases, friendships develop. This living side by side provides many opportunities for inter-religious dialogue. The influential 1991 Vatican document *Dialogue and Proclamation*[6] highlights four distinct kinds of interreligious encounter. Many of these will overlap but the headings are helpful as they clearly show that dialogue with people of other faiths is open to everyone and not just to those with a theological training.

---

6. *Dialogue and Proclamation,* no. 42, www.vatican.va

Firstly, there is the 'dialogue of life' through which people get to know each other as neighbours, at work or through sport or other everyday encounters. They 'live in an open and neighbourly spirit' and share with each other the joys and sorrows of daily life. Monsignor Michael Fitzgerald writes that this form of dialogue is indispensable: 'I would add that these relations, founded on respect, sympathy, even friendship – what the Lebanese are wont to call conviviality – are perhaps the most important, and that the other forms of dialogue ought to serve to reinforce them.'[7] Secondly, there is a 'dialogue of action' through which people of different faiths cooperate for the common good of society through working for a common cause, for example, running a home for the disabled or an organisation to further the rights of women. In this type of encounter, people of goodwill, inspired very often by their own scriptures and religious tradition, will work for justice and peace in order to defend the human dignity of their neighbours, or what in Christian terms we might call 'the bringing in of the Kingdom'. Thirdly, there is the 'dialogue of theological exchange' where suitably qualified theologians seek to deepen their understanding and appreciation of each other's faith and dispel prejudice and misunderstanding, while at the same time respectfully acknowledging their differences. Finally, there is the 'dialogue of religious experience' where people 'share their spiritual riches', their common search for God in their respective prayer and scriptural traditions.

And as the Vatican documents points out, these various forms of dialogue influence each other and overlap:

---

7. Monsignor Michael Fitzgerald, *Dieu rêve d'unité* (Paris: Bayard, 2005), pp. 25–6.

One should not lose sight of this variety of forms of dialogue. Were it to be reduced to theological exchange, dialogue might easily be taken as a sort of luxury item in the Church's mission, a domain reserved for specialists. On the contrary, guided by the Pope and their bishops, all local Churches, and all the members of these Churches, are called to dialogue, though not all in the same way. It can be seen, moreover, that the different forms are interconnected. Contacts in daily life and common commitment to action will normally open the door for cooperation in promoting human and spiritual values; they may also eventually lead to the dialogue of religious experience in response to the great questions which the circumstances of life do not fail to arouse in the minds of people (cf. NA 2).[8] Exchanges at the level of religious experience can give more life to theological discussions. These in turn can enlighten experience and encourage closer contacts.[9]

The different levels of interreligious dialogue outlined above make it clear that it is possible for the non-expert to make a contribution, especially at the level of the dialogue of life founded on friendship. To engage in this form of inter-religious dialogue requires 'an open and neighbourly spirit', a willingness to recognise that, whatever our religious differences, we all share a common humanity.

A CONTINUING DIALOGUE OF FRIENDSHIP
In the second half of this book the focus is exclusively on the

8. *Nostra Aetate:* The Declaration on the Relation of The Church to Non-Christian Religions.
9. *Dialogue and Proclamation*, no. 43.

relationship between the Algerian Church and its Muslim friends. It was my privilege, while writing an account of the lives of the nineteen Algerian martyrs (1994–6),[10] to visit the Algerian Church on two occasions as the guest of Mgr Henri Teissier, Archbishop of Algiers (1998–2008). I was deeply moved by the quality of the relationships that the tiny Christian community had established with its Algerian Muslim brothers and sisters. Part two of this book contains many stories of this continuing dialogue of friendship, encounters where Christians and Muslims, through the working of the Holy Spirit, are enabled to recognise God's presence in each other. These stories of encounter bear witness to the fruitfulness of the Gospel message when it is lived out in all its fullness, and provide examples of all four levels of dialogue, especially of the dialogue of everyday life.

As we seek to explore and reflect upon what we can learn from the North African Church about dialogue and loving our Muslim neighbour, the words of the great Cardinal Duval, Archbishop of Algiers (1954–88) – a person who tirelessly promoted dialogue with Islam – come to mind. He wrote: 'There is no dialogue except among equals. If I think myself superior to my interlocutor, I have only to remain silent. Who can say that before God, the non-Christian to whom I'm speaking isn't superior to me in the homage which he offers to the Creator and in his practice of fraternal love?'[11]

---

10. Martin McGee OSB, *Christian Martyrs for a Muslim People* (New York/Mahwah, NJ: Paulist Press, 2008).
11. *Chemins de Dialogue,* no. 27 (2006), p. 99.

PART I

The Monks of Tibhirine:
Men of Prayer alongside a People of
Prayer

CHAPTER ONE

Pilgrims of Friendship: Notre-Dame de l'Atlas, Morocco

The story of the love of the Tibhirine community for its Muslim neighbours in Algeria has lit a fire that refuses to go out. On 26 March 1996, seven monks from the Trappist monastery of Tibhirine, ninety-six kilometres south of Algiers, were kidnapped by Muslim fundamentalists and fifty-six days later on 21 May all of them were beheaded. There were nine monks present in the monastery on the night of the kidnapping but only seven were taken hostage. Fathers Amédée and Jean-Pierre were overlooked. The Algerian government, fearing for the safety of the monks, refused permission to re-open Tibhirine. There was a short-lived attempt to found a new community at the Nunciature in Algiers. However, with its dissolution, the two survivors joined Tibhirine's small dependent house in Fez, Morocco. On account of the cramped nature of the accommodation, the community decided to relocate and moved in the year 2000 to Midelt, situated one hundred and eighty kilometres south of Fez, a Berber area in the Middle Atlas Mountains.[1]

The inspiring witness of the Tibhirine monks came to the attention of the world thanks to the Xavier Beauvois film

---

1. Apart from five or six Franciscan sisters, there are no other Christians in the region. There are in total about thirty thousand Christians living in Morocco, a country of thirty-three million Muslims. However, the vast majority of the Christian population are foreign workers who will, eventually, go back to their home countries.

Of Gods and Men,[2] winner of the Grand Prix at the Cannes International Film Festival in 2010. This film captured the imagination of countless people, many having little interest in religion or religious affiliation. Why was this? The film focuses on the dilemma facing the monks: should they risk their lives by remaining at Tibhirine in solidarity with their Muslim neighbours and the endangered Christian community? Or should they leave and seek refuge in a safer location? Why did the story of the monks' witness attract over three million viewers in the first eleven weeks of the film's release in France? One reason, I suggest, is that the witness of the monks shows how Christians and Muslims can live together in peace, and even more than that, it shows how they can become brothers and sisters to each other. In a world where Christian–Muslim relations have become tense, especially in the wake of 9/11, this revelation was a moment of insight and hope for many.

One of the main strengths of the film is its careful observation of the close relationship the monks had with the local Muslim villagers. In our present climate of fear and mistrust vis-à-vis Islam, this film helps us to realise that real friendship and love can flourish between Christians and Muslims. This remarkable friendship with their Muslim neighbours was built up over almost sixty years of living cheek by jowl. In their daily life together, the monks and villagers came to recognise and love the presence of God in each other. Father Jean-Pierre, one of the two Tibhirine survivors, remarked in an interview: 'In monastic life one takes a vow of stability which involves promising to remain for the whole of one's life in the monastery. This vow took on a new dimension on account of the ties we had developed with

---

2. *Of Gods and Men* (Des hommes et des dieux) directed by Xavier Beauvois, 2010.

the local population. It was like being married to the people! We would have experienced it as an act of infidelity had we sought refuge whilst leaving our neighbours in disarray.'[3]

THE GRATUITOUS PRESENCE OF GOD'S LOVE

In a homily in Valence, France, to commemorate the tenth anniversary of the martyrdom of the seven Tibhirine monks, Mgr Vincent Landel, Archbishop of Rabat in Morocco, strove to pinpoint the essence of the witness given by the monks of Tibhirine:

> For us, Christians in North Africa, we receive the Lord's invitation to be 'sent into the world', to be just simply this presence of friendship, of respect and welcome, able to live in truth this encounter as a 'sign of God's tenderness for people'. We are invited to live this gratuitous presence of God's love; we are sent into a world of believers and of people of prayer. We do not find this out all at once, but gradually this gives a deeper and deeper meaning to our presence and to our love for the way of life in our countries. Our Trappist brothers [now resident at Midelt in Morocco], very unaffectedly, give us their witness of prayer, friendship, welcome, with the greatest simplicity. Our Trappist brothers are the living witnesses of the message of Tibhirine which gives them life, but which also gives us life. Their discreet and praying presence in North Africa is of paramount importance; without them something of fundamental importance would be missing in our Church.
>
> My predecessor in the See of Rabat liked to say: 'If our North African Church didn't exist, something of the

---

3. *Le Progrès de Lyon,* 20 March 2011.

Catholicity of the Church would be missing.' And yet what are one hundred thousand Catholics, almost all foreigners and temporary residents, doing living in the midst of one hundred million Muslims! We must live the message of Tibhirine throughout North Africa. This message from Tibhirine, you have got to make it real in France and in all of the Catholic Church by welcoming in a spirit of faith, in peace and serenity, the difference of the other who can, in their own way, tell us so many things about God. Amen.[4]

QUALITY OF RELATIONSHIPS

The life of the Midelt community could be described as a life of intense prayer and of dialogue, in the context of daily life, with their Muslim neighbours with whom they have quickly established a very warm and close relationship. However, they are the first to say that their rapid acceptance has been greatly helped by the presence of the Franciscan Sisters who had been in Midelt for seventy-five years before their arrival and had formed a trusting relationship with the local people.

My first visit to the refounded community took place in 2004. Fathers Jean-Pierre and Amédée gave me a very warm welcome and appeared to be particularly happy to receive a monk visitor. Although many religious sisters make retreats at Notre-Dame de l'Atlas, there are few monastic visitors. On the evening of my arrival I was invited to their community meeting at 8 p.m. to introduce myself and to explain the reasons for my visit. I wasn't expecting to have to do this and was a little taken aback. All I could think of saying was that the witness given by the Tibhirine community about the heart of the Gospel message

---

4. Monsignor Vincent Landel, Valence, 4 May 2006, http://catholique-valence.cef.fr

had touched me. In a world where Christian and Muslim are increasingly seen as belonging to opposing camps, they had, through sharing their lives with their Muslim neighbours, broken down the walls of division and mistrust.

During the month of Ramadan the brothers are invited by local families to the evening meal celebrating the end of the daily fast, the Iftar. They, in turn, regularly invite families to a meal in the monastery and attend the funerals and marriages of their neighbours. And every weekday the brothers gather to share some tea with the monastery workers at their morning and afternoon breaks. Paradoxically, these uneducated workmen probably have a much better understanding of the monastic life and the centrality of prayer than many Christian tradesmen in the West. The Muslim appreciation of prayer and worship provides a common meeting ground with the monks.

A Life Centred on Prayer

The Abbot General of the Cistercians, Dom Bernardo Olivera, on meeting the two Tibhirine survivors commented, 'There are two of you. Tibhirine continues.' What is the charism of Tibhirine that flourishes at Midelt today? The charism of Tibhirine is, I think, to be found in the quality of the relationships that the monks have established with their Muslim neighbours. These relationships, however, are founded on a life of prayer.

The Trappists are an eighteenth-century reformed branch of the Cistercians, and their monastic timetable at Midelt is not designed for the faint-hearted. There are seven daily offices to attend, starting with Vigils at 4 a.m. and ending with Compline at 8.30 p.m. The seriousness and devotion with which the monks pray the office seven times a day is striking. Despite being a small and elderly community, three of whom, at the time of my first visit, were eighty years or older, they sang all of the office and gave themselves wholeheartedly to their primary work of prayer. Muslims who pray publicly five times a day easily understand the value of a life centred on prayer. This was the very reason that prompted the late Mgr Hubert Michon, Archbishop of Rabat, to invite the monks of Tibhirine in the 1980s to set up a dependent house in his archdiocese. 'A real spiritual dialogue,' he wrote, could only develop with Muslims if they could see that the Christian community 'contained people of faith and prayer.'[5]

In his Valence homily Mgr Vincent Landel drew attention to the message that the refounded Tibhirine community at Midelt has for us:

> Do we not have to understand more clearly, as our brothers liked to repeat: 'We are people of prayer in the midst of other people of prayer.' What humility is required of us if we are to reach the point of truly believing this: Christians, priests, religious, Trappists, we haven't got a monopoly on this 'heart-to-heart' with God. Our Muslim brothers and sisters are also people of prayer; they are also searching for God; isn't that the whole meaning of the *Ribât*[6] where, starting from the monastery, Christians and Muslims used to meet to deepen their spiritual journey?[7]

---

5. Jean-Pierre Flachaire OCSO, 'Le monastère Notre-Dame de l'Atlas au Maroc', *Collectanea Cisterciensia*, 68:2 (2001), p. 148.

6. The *Ribât* was [and continues to be] an inter-religious group of Christians and Muslims founded by Mgr Claude Rault, a White Father, and Fr Christian of Tibhirine, which met twice a year at Tibhirine to share their search for God and to grow in friendship.

7. http://catholique-valence.cef.fr

A Spiritual Dialogue

Monsignor Vincent is aware of a hardening of the political wing of Islam in recent years. However, while there is not sufficient openness to engage in theological dialogue, he does see openings for spiritual dialogue such as that of the *Ribât* group in Algeria where Christians and Muslims meet twice a year to share their respective spiritual journeys. For the Muslim, according to Mgr Landel, prayer is of the greatest importance. Those who pray are much more respected than those who don't. In this regard it's worth quoting again Mgr Landel's homily at Valence:

> In the Priory of Notre-Dame de l'Atlas at Midelt, our brothers Jean-Pierre (the younger), Jean-Pierre (the elder), Amédée and Louis, while remembering what has gone before, wish to continue to live out this message of Tibhirine. They wish to pursue their commitment to be 'praying Christians, pilgrims of friendship, in this Muslim world'. They are at the beginning of the foundation, but, little by little, friendships are being made; prayer is becoming the bond that brings them life. You should have seen the pride of Omar, one of their workers, when he, with such delicacy, embellished the monastery chapel. The prayer of the brothers is of the utmost importance. Thus, at the heart of their common vocation to adore God, to praise him and to sing his glory, each person respects the other and esteems the other. As one of them wrote: 'Fidelity to the rendezvous of prayer is the secret of our friendship with the Muslims. With them we wish to come into God's presence, to be true to ourselves in this interior light which silence permits.'

Thus among the Muslims, who are their first and almost only neighbours, they are the forerunners of the dialogue of friendship; they are the sign of the encounter which can take place in the light of faith in the one God.[8]

Following my first visit to Midelt in 2004 I returned on five occasions, drawn by the hospitality and prayer of this tiny community. During my six visits I met a community and a Church at the service of the dialogue of daily life, sharing their search for God in prayer with a people of prayer, and thereby sowing seeds of reconciliation and hope for the future. In the midst of so much mistrust between Islam and Christianity it is heart-warming to see how friendships grow when people take the trouble to live side by side in a spirit of peace and prayer.

---

8. Ibid.

CHAPTER TWO

Father Jean-Pierre: Happiness is Found in Relationships

Perhaps what most moved viewers of the film *Of Gods and Men* was the quality of the relationships between the monks and their Muslim neighbours. The media tends to focus only on the growing mistrust between Muslims and Christians; whereas in the film we learn about the growing love and understanding which developed between the monks and their neighbours as they got to know each other better. And the greatest witness of the monks, and of the North African Church today, continues to lie in the quality of the relationships that they have developed with their Muslim neighbours.

Many of us living in the developed countries of the West, for one reason or another, remain distant from our Muslim neighbours. Unless we are young and meet them at school, the only other place where people tend to interact is in the workplace. Socially we tend to inhabit separates worlds. That is, at least my impression, living in Britain today. However, the monks of Tibhirine and the tiny Christian minorities in North Africa, as they are few in number and no longer hold any of the levers of power in society, don't have any option but to mix with and get to know their Muslim neighbours. It is in this context of weakness and vulnerability that real relationships of equality and friendship have flourished. The first and most important step in inter-religious dialogue is to get to know the other, to become a good neighbour.

The life of Jean-Pierre Schumacher,[1] one of the two Tibhirine monks who escaped the kidnappers on 26 March 1996 is the story of such a journey of friendship. In his recently published autobiographical reflections *L'esprit de Tibhirine*,[2] Fr Jean-Pierre tells us the secret of 'the dialogue of friendship'. Father Jean-Pierre, the eldest of six children, was born on 14 February 1924, into a devout Catholic family in the little village of Buding, in Lorraine, France. His family had been millers for many generations. As a boy he enjoyed serving at Mass and had a good relationship with the parish priest. He also enjoyed excellent relations with the Marist Fathers who ran the boarding school he attended. There was no corporal punishment and the priests were very close to the students. So the choice for him, unsurprisingly, was between becoming a priest or a miller.

One other feature of life in the village was the excellent relationship between the villagers and the local Jewish community. Jean-Pierre's best friend at primary school, Sylvain, was Jewish and the outstanding student in his secondary school class was also a Jewish boy. So it came as a great shock when Jean-Pierre learned after the war that some relatives of this student had been deported and murdered by the Nazis. After celebrating his first Mass in his native village, he was very moved when a local Jewish woman came out of her house to congratulate him. All of these positive experiences were undoubtedly preparing him for his later encounters with that other great monotheistic faith, Islam.

---

1. Father Amédée, the other survivor, died in 2008.
2. Frère Jean-Pierre et Nicolas Ballet, *L'esprit de Tibhirine* (Paris: Éditions du Seuil, 2012).

AN ATTRACTION TO THE CONTEMPLATIVE LIFE

Given Jean-Pierre's positive experience of being educated by the Marists, it's not surprising that, after some hesitation, he joined that order and was duly ordained as a priest. Jean-Pierre, however, had for a long time harboured a longing for the contemplative life, a life where he felt he could give himself more fully to God. His wish to join a contemplative monastery was eventually acceded to by the Marist order. However, he left the choice of monastery to his superiors and so he ended up joining the Trappist monastery of Timadeuc in Brittany in 1955 at the age of thirty-one. He thought that he would spend the rest of his life there. To his surprise, seven years later in 1964, he was designated, along with three other monks of Timadeuc, to go to Algeria to support the community at Tibhirine. The monastery was much depleted in numbers at the time, having just four monks. Father Jean-Pierre was delighted to have been chosen. He had been influenced by the opening to the outside world occasioned by the Second Vatican Council. Although only 'on loan' to Tibhirine, this was, as far as he was concerned, a commitment for life. 'I had made up my mind to remain for good and to live the experience of a small community in the spirit of Vatican II vis-à-vis Islam. Such an experience excited me.'[3]

ENCULTURATION AT TIBHIRINE

Father Jean-Pierre arrived at Tibhirine on 19 September 1964. From 1962 until 1984 Tibhirine had a succession of temporary superiors giving rise to a time of instability as each new superior had a different way of leading the community. Finally in 1984 the community had a sufficient number of monks permanently

---

3. The interviews with Fr Jean-Pierre and Fr Amédée were conducted by me in French in Midelt, Morocco, in July 2007.

settled at Tibhirine to enable them to elect their own superior. They decided not to elect an abbot but a prior, as this was better suited to the modest size of the community.

The new prior was Dom Christian de Chergé, a gifted monk who was committed to the Algerian Church and people. Father Christian had studied Arabic and Islamology for two years in Rome and was keen to engage in dialogue with the local culture and religion. Christian was keen to integrate the community more deeply into the culture of their adopted country. For example, Jean-Pierre recounts that he proposed that those monks who wished to master Arabic should say the office of tierce in Arabic in the guesthouse. This proposal wasn't accepted as it was felt that it would divide the community. The Our Father and a few Marian antiphons in Arabic were introduced into the liturgy but the majority of the monks were against introducing Muslim texts as they felt this would be disrespectful to the local people and would also be unfaithful to their own tradition. Where Fr Christian did make progress was in the foundation of the *Ribât*, a group of Christians and Sufis who sought to share their spiritual search for God whilst respecting each other's tradition. Three of the monks – Christian, Michel and Christophe – became full members of this group. The spiritual sharing in the *Ribât* did not involve theological dialogue where the thorny issues of the Trinity, the divinity of Jesus and the nature of revelation could quickly lead to an impasse.

The monks were very clear about the distinction between spiritual sharing and theological discussion. As Fr Amédée told me in Morocco:

In my daily contacts there are never any theological discussions. Our relations with our neighbours are a relationship of friendship, of mutual understanding, of accepting ourselves as different, but we never start discussing theological issues. Sometimes Fr Christophe had spiritual discussions in the garden, for example, about morality ... but that's totally different from a theological discussion! Thus many young people liked to talk to Fr Christophe especially about prayer, spirituality, but not about theology which would cause them to doubt their faith.

REMAINING TRULY WHAT ONE IS

Father Jean-Pierre recounts that at first he felt he should follow the example of St Paul who wrote: 'To the Jews I became as a Jew, in order to win Jews. To those under the law I became as one under the law (though I myself am not under the law) so that I might win those under the law' (1 Cor 9:20). But he came to see the difficulties of this ambition as time passed.

We thought that we should draw near to them as much as possible in their manner of life, of dress, learn the language of course, and even take their nationality. With this in mind the community considered re-ordering the Chapel to face east following the Muslim tradition. But then after reflection they concluded: No. The Church has the altar in the centre with the congregation around it and Christ in the centre. We're not orientated towards a cardinal point, we're orientated towards Christ and one should be able to notice this as soon as one enters the church, to be able to understand the mystery of the church. ... We realised that it's not a question of being Muslim with Muslims and Greek with the Greeks. It was necessary to remain what one was: foreigner, French, Christian, monk, and to be accepted as such by people. And as for us, to love them as they are. Inter-religious dialogue is about remaining truly what one is and not looking to soften the edges where they exist; to show things as they are, to succeed in making oneself understood and accepted as one is, to cultivate what we hold in common.

These tensions within the community didn't imply that Frs Jean-Pierre, Amédée and Br Luc weren't as keen as Fr Christian on inter-religious dialogue with their Muslim neighbours. They wanted to live alongside them as brothers sharing a common Father and a common humanity. They wanted to serve them lovingly and in this way for both sides to draw closer to the one Father of all mankind. They very much shared in the Algerian Church's concept of being a sacrament of God's presence, a visible sign of God's love for each other. In talking about his work as the community's 'shopper' three times a week in the local town of Médéa, where he also sold the monastery's produce at the market, Fr Jean-Pierre said that he wasn't particularly gifted for this kind of work. What he did love about it was the fact that it enabled him to be a Christian presence among them, someone who showed them Christ's love. 'This was part of my missionary vocation, to be a presence of the monastery among them. I bought, I sold, I had the same difficulties as they did, the same battles to fight as they did.'

Father Jean-Pierre remembers a religious sister telling him that when she asked the locals whether they should make a foundation in Algeria, they replied: 'If you're coming here to do things, some kind or other of charitable work, no, we don't need you. If you're coming to live among us, Yes, do come.' The monastery is there to be faithful to its monastic charism but also, as Fr Jean-Pierre said to the General Chapter of the Trappist Order, it is there:

for the Muslims, its fellow human beings. This little preposition 'for' hasn't much importance, has only three letters, but everything is contained in them. It gives the tone: a whole way of being to be discovered and lived, an appropriate equilibrium between separation from the world and presence to the world, not easy to achieve but indispensable so that the current might pass in both directions, a current which must be that of the Holy Spirit accomplishing his work in both parties, an osmosis of that which is best in each one, a gift of God which comes from elsewhere.[4]

A COMMON SEARCH FOR GOD

Father Jean-Pierre's favourite image to describe the silent prayer and fellowship that they shared with the Sufis – an ascetic, mystical branch of Islam – in the *Ribât* is that of a ladder with two sides. This was described by one of the Sufi participants as follows: 'You climb by one of the sides towards God. We climb by the other. The closer one comes to the top of this ladder towards heaven, the closer one comes to each other. And the closer one comes to each other, the closer one is to God.'[5] Jean-Pierre isn't afraid to say that, at times, he feels that he has a more fraternal relationship with the Sufis than with certain Christians 'because this relationship between us was begun under the impulse of the Holy Spirit and because this relationship involved an authentic [spiritual] sharing'.[6] Father Jean-Pierre, like Amédée before him, refuses to become involved in theological disputes about the Trinity or the divinity of Jesus. And that explains why the

---

4. Talk given by Fr Jean-Pierre in 1996 to the General Chapter of the Trappists in Rome.
5. Frère Jean-Pierre et Nicolas Ballet, pp. 166–7.
6. Ibid., p. 167.

spiritual friendship and sharing with the Sufis were so fruitful because both sides avoided theological issues and focused instead on sharing the common search for God in prayer and everyday life. This approach is very congenial to the Rule of St Benedict, which also focuses more on the search for God in everyday life than on doctrinal exploration. Jean-Pierre likes to say, following Fr Christian, that 'the best Muslim is the person who is the most submitted to God and that Christ is the best Muslim because he is One with the Father'.[7]

In his recent book, *L'esprit de Tibhirine*, Fr Jean-Pierre remarks that the West, since the fall of the communist bloc in 1991, has found 'a new enemy', namely radical Islamism. In the present climate of fear and distrust it is very easy for us to demonise the other who is different. He writes: 'Similar to any other religion, Islam is not the incarnation of violence. In the name of what or whom, moreover, have we the right to burden a certain part of the population, or a certain religious tradition, with every ill?'[8] Father Jean-Pierre is aware of doctrinal and political obstacles on the path of mutual understanding and respect. And, of course, as we are all aware, it is easy to dwell on the speck in our brother's eye and to fail to see the log in our own. In this regard Fr Michel Guillaud, a priest of the diocese of Constantine in Algeria, remarked that it is very easy for us to present 'Islam by its shadows and Christianity by its lights'. He goes on to say that 'we still have to make a great effort to recognise what is beautiful in the other tradition, to be able to understand, respect, esteem the spiritual élan of the other and of particular people or aspects of their religion'.[9]

---

7. Ibid., p. 171.
8. Ibid., p. 180.
9. *L'Écho du diocèse de Constantine et d'Hippone*, Septembre–Octobre, no. 4, (2012), p. 15.

For Fr Jean-Pierre the key and most fundamental way of engaging in dialogue rests at the level of everyday life. After forty-eight years of living in the Maghreb, Fr Jean-Pierre is convinced that the real answer to our misunderstandings and fears is to be found in this form of dialogue, even when confronted by 'radical Islamism'. 'Conviviality and friendship are more valuable than all the fine speeches in the world. It is lived experiences that allow bonds to be developed, beyond differences. Happiness is found in relationships – relationships with the other and relationships with God.'[10]

And this form of dialogue, the dialogue of friendship, is open to all of us. The only qualification required is that we try to see and love God's image and likeness in our neighbour.

---

10. Frère Jean-Pierre et Nicolas Ballet, p. 198.

CHAPTER THREE

Brother Luc: The Impact of Sanctity

The greatest 'proof' that God exists and the greatest 'proof' of the indwelling of the Holy Spirit in another faith tradition is shown when we meet a person who loves, a person who embodies in the little acts of everyday life God's loving presence; for as St John teaches us 'God is love.' When we meet such a person, everything changes and our preconceptions and prejudices begin to crumble. The Second Vatican Council in its decree on ecumenism states that personal holiness is at the heart of ecumenism. It is likewise at the heart of inter-religious dialogue. This can be seen in the impact that the holiness of Br Luc had on his Muslim neighbours. If one picture is worth a thousand words, in inter-religious dialogue one loving act of kindness is equally effective. That is why the life of Br Luc was so powerful in breaking down barriers between the monks and their Muslim neighbours. It is a life that speaks to us powerfully about loving our Muslim neighbours.

CLOTHED AS A LAY BROTHER
As a result of the film *Of Gods and Men,* Br Luc of Tibhirine has become a well-known figure, at least throughout the French-speaking world. Before his martyrdom, in the Algerian civil war in 1996, he was completely unknown, his life in the words of St Paul 'being hidden with Christ in God' (Col 3:3). Paul Dochier, Br Luc in monastic life, was born on 31 January 1914 in Bourg-de-Péage in the Drôme, the third child of Gabriel Dochier

and Hélène Ageron.[1] At secondary school he was a fanatical rugby player so much so that his studies suffered and he was obliged to repeat his baccalaureate, which he did successfully. He started his medical studies at Lyon in 1932 where he proved to be a brilliant student. His first contact with monastic life occurred when he visited the Trappist Abbey of Aiguebelle in 1937. He wanted to give up his medical studies there and then but the abbot counselled him to finish his studies before joining the novitiate. Although attracted by the Carthusian life, Luc entered the abbey of Aiguebelle in November 1941, having qualified as a medical doctor in 1940.

In the summer of 1943, on hearing that a doctor from his native village, and father of four children, was a prisoner of war in Germany, Br Luc volunteered to replace him. In the oflag, a camp for officers, he worked as a doctor going out of his way to care for the Russian prisoners who were being harshly treated. On being released in 1945 he returned, after a short period of convalescence, to the monastery of Aiguebelle and on 15 August 1946 he made his simple profession as a lay brother. Less than two weeks later he set out with some other monks from Aiguebelle to strengthen the Trappist foundation at Tibhirine[2] in Algeria.

---

1. Most of the biographical details have been taken from Christophe Henning, Dom Thomas Georgeon, *Frère Luc, la biographie* (Montrouge: Bayard Éditions, 2011) or from interviews which I conducted in French with Fr Jean-Pierre Schumacher, a monk of Tibhirine, at the monastery of Notre-Dame de l'Atlas, Midelt, Morocco, in July 2007.
2. An account of life at Tibhirine and of the martyrdom of the other eighteen priests and religious in Algeria in the 1990s can be found in my book, Martin McGee OSB, *Christian Martyrs for a Muslim People* (New York/Mahwah NJ: Paulist Press, 2008).

GENUINE FRIENDSHIP WITH THE POOR

The monastery of Notre-Dame de l'Atlas was situated ninety-six kilometres south of Algiers, and the surrounding area was very poor with no medical services. A Tibhirine monk and herbalist, Fr Berchmans, had been providing some medical assistance in a dispensary run by the monastery. The poverty and lack of medical care came as a shock to Br Luc who, on his arrival, discovered that five children had just died from measles. Within a few weeks Br Luc was already engaged in working in the dispensary. An old sick woman said to him: 'But why are you coming to look after me? You're not a relative. Why? I thank you with all my heart.'[3]

Right from the start Br Luc was able to establish a very close relationship with the poor of the surrounding countryside, a relationship that fulfilled him. Women in particular appreciated his presence as it afforded them an opportunity to leave the stifling confines of the family home and pour out their troubles to a sympathetic ear. They knew they could trust Br Luc with their confidences and problems. Br Luc, while obviously valuing the medical help that he provided for the villagers, was also acutely aware of the spiritual importance of his work. He wrote: 'The purpose of this dispensary is not so much to promote bodily well-being and the maximum of medical efficiency as to show love towards a poor and unfortunate people by means of a genuine friendship.'[4] His powers of diagnosis and his understanding of his patients' social and religious background ensured that he had a constant and never-ending stream of patients waiting to see him. With up to seventy consultations a day, all free of charge, his life was extremely busy.

---

3. Henning and Georgeon, p. 34.
4. Ibid., p. 46.

In the Act of Giving We Find Life

As the New Testament makes very clear the one non-negotiable criterion by which a person's life will be judged is the commandment of love, love of God which manifests itself in love of neighbour. Every Christian and every saint's life gives witness to love in its many and varied forms. For without love the Christian life bears no lasting fruit. Although as a lay brother he was a little outside the life of the community – he didn't attend the office or community meetings – nevertheless he served it in a very concrete manner. In addition to his taxing work as a doctor, he was also the part-time monastery cook, sharing this position with Br Michel. This meant that on his duty days he had to get up as early as 2 a.m. in order to prepare the food in advance. Living cheek by jowl for years on end means that monks get to know very well each other's strengths and weaknesses. And maintaining good relationships with everyone in such confined circumstances, as Br Luc did, can be very demanding.

Brother Luc was aware of his weaknesses of character but he was also full of hope. 'The person who walks the Christian way recognises his sin, and yet he doesn't despair because he knows that the Spirit continues his work within him and leads him by the hand, very gently, towards the Father's house.'[5] Brother Luc had no illusions about either his own weaknesses or about those of others. He knew that what counted in life was our ability to love without looking for a payback. 'If the other does not respond, that's of no importance, it's in the very act of giving that we find "life".'[6]

---

5. Ibid., p. 146.
6. Ibid., p. 186.

An Everyday Saint

Brother Luc was what might be called an everyday saint in that he worked with the challenges and suffering with which daily life presented him. I think it's true to say that all saints bear deeply in their lives the marks of the cross. It's not that they search out suffering, but rather that they are more willing than those of us in the foothills of Christian discipleship to take up the cross in the service of love. His life was not without its share of tension, struggle and pain. He had to combine a very demanding schedule of work in the dispensary and in the kitchen. In addition his asthma, which he developed while in the German prisoner of war camp, became an ever greater burden. Also, in July 1959 during the Algerian War of Independence, Br Luc and Br Matthieu were kidnapped for ten days, a precursor of the fatal kidnapping in 1996.

Brother Luc was the only Tibhirine monk to wear his habit daily, even when visiting the local town of Médéa, an Islamic stronghold. The local people accepted this as they regarded him as a *marabout* or holy man. They could see that his service of the poor Muslims of Tibhirine and of his brothers in the community was done willingly and out of love and they loved him in return. This was the real secret of the radiance of Tibhirine and of its ability to break down the barriers of suspicion and prejudice, to engage in inter-religious dialogue of the heart. The devout Muslim villagers, none of them theologically educated, could see that the monks were men of prayer who fasted, gave alms and served each other in their own community and who also served them with equal love and devotion.

He Loved Them for Themselves

As Fr Christian once remarked 'the villagers had never heard of Cistercians, Trappists, or even monks. The villagers had no need of such esoteric labels but were quite clear about the identity of the brothers. They were simply *roumis*, i.e. Christians. The *roumis* in their case, according to Fr Christian, would be understood in terms of the villagers' own religious practice as a person who "prays, believes in God, fasts and gives to the poor … he is almost like one of us!"[7] Brother Luc excelled in humble service of his neighbour – whether Muslim or Christian made no difference to him. As a follower of the Rule of St Benedict he had penetrated the core of its Gospel spirituality, namely, the practice of humility. And, of course, Benedictine monasticism, with its emphasis on obedience to God's will and on human insignificance before God – or humility – resonates strongly with the teaching of the Qur'an. And that is why monks are in a privileged position to carry on dialogue with Islam. In 1976 Br Luc wrote during the community retreat: 'The day when I accept with joy that people say about me, "He's very ordinary", that's the day when I shall be truly humble, on that day I'll give thanks to God that his leaven and his power … appear to have put within my reach the bread of life. And on that day I'll be able to become, even in solitude, "the man for others".'[8]

As death drew near, Br Luc wrote in 1994: 'My only trust, my only hope is the infinite mercy of God who welcomes each one of us as we are. Despite the misfortunes of life, it's a grace to have been born, because at the heart of adversity there is someone. The secret of life is to LOVE.'[9] Brother Luc had taken to heart Jesus' parable of the Last Judgement in Matthew's Gospel that we would be judged on our loving service of our neighbour regardless of their religious or racial identity. And his Muslim

---

7. McGee, p. 80.

8. Henning and Georgeon, pp. 110-111.

9. Georgeon, p. 225.

neighbours knew that Br Luc loved them for themselves; he wasn't fulfilling a duty to love but expressing the love of the Holy Spirit that dwelt in him. 'God is love' and where love is active barriers of mistrust and prejudice are dismantled, minds and hearts are opened, and people begin to see God's presence in each other and in each other's religion.

Brother Luc led a hidden life at Tibhirine. Through a quirk of fate, or providence if you wish, his impact is no longer confined to the villagers of Tibhirine but has rippled out across the world through the film *Of Gods and Men*. No doubt Br Luc would not have seen himself as a great force for bringing Muslims and Christians closer together. He would rather have seen himself as someone called to love, as Jesus loved, the least of his brothers and sisters. That, as Br Luc reminds us, is the secret of holiness and Gospel living and the most powerful way of breaking down barriers in inter-religious dialogue.

CHAPTER FOUR

Brother Michel: A Lover of the Muslim Soul

Brother Michel exemplified the ideal of the monastic life, a hidden life of prayer, silence, work and community life. He had no intellectual pretensions but sought, in the steps of St Benedict, to deepen his relationship with Christ through the pondering of God's Word in scripture. Brother Michel was known for his love of silence, an indispensable gift for deepening our ability to hear and assimilate the Word of God. Brother Michel was a monk in probably the poorest and most vulnerable Trappist monastery in the world – financially weak, fragile in vocations and totally dependent on the goodwill of its Muslim neighbours.

Through fidelity to his monastic vocation, Br Michel was enabled also to enter more deeply into the Muslim soul and thus become in his own quiet and hidden way a person of dialogue, exemplifying the saying that as we grow closer to God we also grow closer to our neighbour. And Br Michel's only neighbours during his time at Tibhirine were Muslims, apart from a few Christian retreatants in the monastery guest house. Following his death, several personal reflections were found which reveal the inner man caught up by the love of God. And these testimonies, along with some letters to his family and monastic friends, have enabled us to get to know him better and to account for his impact on the villagers of Tibhirine. Like Br Luc, Br Michel's life spoke more by his example and silence than by his words.

DRAWN TO THE WORLD OF ISLAM

Brother Michel Fleury[1] was born on 21 May 1944 in France in the village of Cotteret in the Loire-Atlantique. His parents were farmers and he had one older brother and a younger sister. When he was seventeen he felt a call to the priesthood and in 1966 entered the major seminary at Nantes where he completed four years of studies, one of which involved a year's work experience in a factory. He decided, however, that his vocation lay elsewhere and in 1971 he joined the Prado Institute in Lyons as a brother. This was a society of priests founded by Antoine Chevrier to work among the urban working class. In his work as a machine operator in a local factory he came into contact with North African immigrants, and also, as he learned to study and pray the scriptures, he came under the influence of Père Chevrier's foundational book *Le Véritable Disciple* (The True Disciple). Thanks to Père Chevrier, he acquired a love of the Word of God that would nourish him for the rest of his life. From 1976 onwards, he began to feel dissatisfied with his life at the Prado, eventually leaving in November 1980 to join the Trappist community of Bellefontaine.

Brother Michel had come to know well the Muslim world in France, having lived for a year as a member of the Prado in a hostel for Muslim immigrants and also having worked in a Marseilles factory, from 1975 to 1979, where many of his fellow workers would have been of North African origin. So it's not really surprising that he should feel the call to join the Tibhirine community ninety-six kilometres south of Algiers that drew its

---

1. Most of the biographical details have been taken from interviews which I conducted in French with Fr Jean-Pierre Schumacher, a monk of Tibhirine, at the monastery of Notre-Dame de l'Atlas, Midelt, Morocco, in July 2007 or from http://www.moinestibhirine.org

members from French Trappist monasteries. The recruitment of monks in Algeria wasn't possible as there was only a tiny resident Christian community following the departure, in the aftermath of independence in 1962, of the vast majority of the European settlers. Brother Michel arrived at Tibhirine on 28 August 1984 – the feast day of St Augustine, Algeria's most famous saint – and made his solemn vows there on the same feast day in 1986. Although he had no special aptitude for cooking, he was asked to work in the kitchen, a task he accepted out of obedience. In the words of Fr Jean-Pierre, this change of monastic stability was a continuation of what he had sought at Bellefontaine, 'a hidden life, offered in silence, for the Algerians'.[2]

A Life Freely Given

Fortuitously, a few of Br Michel's spiritual testimonies were discovered following his death, allowing us to glimpse the depth of his inner life.[3] The first is a short act of self-oblation that Fr Jean-Pierre Flachaire discovered on a postcard while leafing through a book in the library at Tibhirine. This was written at Pentecost in 1993, a time when violence was spreading its tentacles and coming closer and closer to the monastery with each passing day. Brother Michel knew in his heart that a violent death was a real possibility and so he wrote a prayer of self-offering to the Holy Spirit. No one would take his life. It would be freely given:

2. This and subsequent quotations of Fr Jean-Pierre are taken from interviews which I conducted in French with him at the monastery of Notre-Dame de l'Atlas, Midelt, Morocco, in July 2007.

3. The original French version of these testimonies can be found in an article by Étienne Baudry OCSO, 'Itinéraire spirituel du frère Michel Fleury, moine de Tibhirine', *Collectanea Cisterciensia*, 63: 3 (2001), pp. 264–83. The English translations are my own.

Holy Spirit Creator, deign to associate me, and as quickly as possible, not my will but yours, with the Paschal Mystery of Jesus Christ our Lord in whatever way you wish, certain that You, Lord Jesus, You will live it in me – and for whatever reason you wish, in imitation of Mary and the Apostles. Deign to receive this poor offering of your unworthy servant (Jn 15:12-16) … and 'friend' Michel, to the praise of your glory, and consume it in the fire of your Love.
O You who lives in the communion of the Father and the Son, to you praise and glory eternally.
Made on this blessed day of Pentecost 30 May 1993
N.B. Eve of the feast of the Visitation and of the Aïd-el-Kbir.[4]
Br Michel the m [sic].

On reading this act of total self-oblation in union with Jesus on the cross we can sense the profound faith and humility of Br Michel. He signed his self-offering 'Br Michel the m.', the 'm' probably standing for 'martyr'. Brother Michel, like the rest of the monks, didn't know for certain that he would be asked to make the supreme sacrifice of laying down his life for his friends but his intuition, as evident in this prayer, told him that this was likely to happen.

I HAVE NO STRENGTH
In fact, on Christmas Eve 1993 the community had what might be described as a dress rehearsal for their eventual martyrdom. On that evening a group of armed 'brothers of the mountain'

---

4. This Islamic Feast of the Sacrifice commemorates Abraham's obedience to God by his willingness to sacrifice Ishmael [sic].

invaded the cloisters and demanded to speak to the 'pope', i.e., Fr Christian, the prior. The leader of the Islamic group, Sayah Attia, had slit the throats of twelve Christian Croatian building workers a few days earlier on 15 December at Tamesguida about five kilometres from the monastery. The monks, who knew these workers, thought that their turn had now come.

Father Jean-Pierre recounts that Br Célestin and himself were being taken by a young armed man in military uniform to the guest house where Sayah Attia was waiting. Brother Michel appeared at this instant and was summoned to join them.

> We thought that it was our turn, that our death was close. Michel followed without saying a word, meekly. I thought of the text from Isaiah, 'like a lamb that is led to the slaughter … he did not open his mouth' (53:7). This text, applied to Jesus in the liturgy, tells us something about what Michel's attitude must have been on the night of the kidnapping, 26 March 1996, and during the time which passed until his death. He was ready, he was offered by the same Spirit that made him leave the Prado to enter the Trappists, then to leave Bellefontaine to come to Algeria. *El hamdoulilah* – praise to you, God – into your hands, Lord!

However, this prayer of self-sacrifice and the reality of the extreme tension under which the monks were living took its toll. On 28 January 1994, just a month after the invasion of the monastery, Fr Christophe notes in his diary the impact all these events have had on Br Michel. 'Michel, yesterday morning. Passing the mop, he stops and looks up at me with his limpid gaze to utter, barely opening his mouth: "It's not like it used to be. Since they came, I have no strength."[5] Dom Bernardo, Abbot General of the Trappists, reminds us that Br Michel would now have to live out 'the text he had written for his [temporary] profession: "My grace is sufficient for you, for my power is made perfect in weakness"(2 Cor 12:9)'.[6]

ANOINTED BY GOD'S WORD

The next document that gives us an insight into Br Michel's state of mind is a letter which he wrote sometime in August 1994 to his priest cousin in France, Joseph Crand, expressing his wonder at God's active presence in his life. Brother Michel reflects on the prospect of martyrdom and its ambiguity in a country where Islamic gunmen were more than willing to sacrifice their lives to further their cause. He also rejoices in the strength the Lord has given him through a passage from St Paul.

> ... 'Martyr' is such an ambiguous word here. If something should happen to us – I don't want it to – we wish to live it here in solidarity with all these Algerian men and women who have already paid with their lives ... It seems to me that he who is helping us today to persevere, it is he who has called us. *I remain full of wonder*: 'But it is God who establishes us with you [the Algerian people] in Christ and has anointed us, by putting his seal on us and giving us his Spirit in our hearts as a first instalment' (2 Cor 1:21-22). A word of St Paul which was given to me during the Liturgy of the Hours on the feast of Corpus Christi, following a community reflection on the events of 8 May [the assassination of Sr

---

5. Baudry, p. 270.
6. Bernardo Olivera OCSO, 'Tibhirine Today', Circular Letter, Rome, 21 May 2006, p. 9.

Paul-Hélène and Br Henri Vergès, the first of the nineteen religious to be assassinated in Algeria], a Word which still speaks to me, giving me the strength to live *peacefully* today with my brothers. There's nothing of a hero about me and *everything of a zero*.[7]

With the assassination of Sr Paul-Hélène and Br Henri Vergès the noose was tightening and the ambient violence was drawing ever closer to the community. Father Michel was aware of the risks and had no wish to seek out death. In the same letter to his cousin he writes: 'It's certain that if we were directly threatened we would leave.' Above all, Br Michel is aware of his own lack of courage, his own spiritual poverty in the face of the surrounding violence and hatred. However, his surprise and joy are great when he experiences the strength of God's Word anointing him in the Holy Spirit. In a letter to the Abbot of Bellefontaine, written in the same month, he comments that he has never known the Word of God to speak so powerfully to him daily, encouraging him to continue in his monastic life at Tibhirine. Peace and wonder are his lot.

His Word Was a Lamp for My Feet

Père Amédée discovered a final posthumous message from Br Michel on a scrap of paper among his books and papers. His brief and unsentimental spiritual testament shows us someone who was ready to make the supreme sacrifice of his life in a calm and peaceful manner. His life had become totally conformed to that of his Master.

1.   Burn everything you find written by me, as well as certain unusable books, etc.

---

7.   Baudry, p. 271.

2. Marie-France, Louis [his brother & sister]: please do not reproach in any way my superior and brothers in the community because in faith 'His Word was a lamp for my feet.'

3. For my funeral mass, follow the readings of the day because 'His Word was a lamp for my feet and a light to my path.' Don't forget the Magnificat.

   Long live God, Long live the Church, Long live Algeria. Goodbye. See you soon.

   The feast of the Assumption of the Virgin Mary, 15.08.95

   Br Michel

   N.B. Pray to the God of Mercy for the forgiveness of all my sins.

   And GIVE THANKS to the Lord for He is GOOD.

This simple testament sums up Br Michel's monastic life. Firstly, there is his humility. He doesn't wish to be remembered or made a fuss of. He requests that all his personal writings be destroyed. He doesn't want any attention drawn to himself and asks that his family should not hold his monastic community in any way responsible for his death. And he also asks his family to pray for his own sinfulness. Brother Michel knew well his own strengths and weaknesses, that self-knowledge which is the seedbed of humility.

Secondly, his love of God's Word shines forth, a Word that nourished him daily and gave him the strength to persevere calmly in the face of death. God's Word, as he remarked in his letter to his cousin, had anointed him in the Spirit, strengthening him to bear peacefully the time of testing which he and the Tibhirine community were facing. Brother Michel's love of the monastic practice of *lectio divina,* the prayerful pondering of the scriptures, had borne a rich harvest.

Thirdly, his love of his Algerian neighbours is present. *Vive l'Algérie.* He had a strong relationship with the Muslim families who worked alongside the monks in the monastic orchard and vegetable garden.

The Search for the Muslim Soul

Brother Michel was (with Fr Christian) one of only two monks who took a full part in the *Ribât* right from the start.[8] The *Ribât* was a group of Christian and Muslim seekers who met in the monastery for a weekend every six months to share their spiritual struggles and insights. Although he had no aptitude for learning Arabic, Fr Jean-Pierre told me that Br Michel was greatly attracted by Muslim spirituality as found in Sufi texts.

> He sometimes quoted extracts from these writings as part of his intercessory prayer at the Divine Office or at Mass. The presence of the Sufi confraternity, the *'Alawiyya*, one day in three at the meetings of the *Ribât*; the common prayer with them, often in silence, the sharing on a chosen theme; all this sustained his expectations and hopes. It seems that his perspective on Islam was nourished principally by this type of encounter, as a road towards God on which we can walk some way together in a mutually enriching solidarity.

> Having fractured his arm after falling from a ladder, he had to regularly visit the hospital for physiotherapy sessions. He used to take along a book, *La Rose de l'Imam,*[9] to pass the time

---

8. Father Christophe would become a full member shortly before his assassination in 1996.
9. Marius Garau, *La Rose de l'Imam* (Paris: Collection 'Rencontres Islam', Éditions du Cerf, 1983).

in the waiting room. The author, Marius Garau, recounts his special relationship with an imam. They had engaged together in a search for God and a discovery of each other in depth, in a spirit of respect, admiration and praise. Michel liked this approach very much. It seems evident to me that his search for God in the monastery was inseparably linked to his search for the Muslim soul in order to walk alongside it and to offer himself for it. Some people thought he had an aura of sanctity; I wonder if he was aware of this? The workers in the garden liked him and respected him. He knew how, at the appropriate moment, to give them a share of the fruit and vegetables for their families in whom he showed an interest.

In a letter to his cousins shortly before his death, Br Michel asked them to pray that the monks who had 'been called to live the Mystery of the Covenant with the Algerian people'[10] would remain faithful to their commitment. For Br Michel his life alongside the villagers was an expression of his own covenanted relationship with God in Jesus Christ.

While on a visit to his family in France, Br Michel's nephew, knowing the danger he was in, had twice asked him if he was going to return to Algeria. And Br Michel had replied: 'Yes.' In a letter to his priest cousin Joseph Crand, he asked him to 'pray that the Spirit might make him [his nephew] understand this simple yes'.[11] This 'simple yes' to the Spirit sums up the depth of Br Michel's love for God, for the Church and for Algeria.

Undoubtedly the monastic way of life with its demand for silence and meditating upon the Word of God is a particularly good formation for someone undertaking inter-religious

10. Baudry, p. 275.
11. Ibid., p. 280.

dialogue. The ability to listen, to enter into a deeper relationship with God's Word, enables the person to engage in a dialogue of the heart that takes one beyond difference. In the silence of his heart a space opened up where Br Michel could glimpse the image and likeness of God in his Muslim brothers and sisters. That same space is also there for us to explore.

CHAPTER FIVE

Father Christian: Discovering God's Presence in Each Other

Father Christian de Chergé, the prior or superior of the Tibhirine monastic community, is undoubtedly the best known of the seven monk martyrs. The posthumous publication of his spiritual *Testament*,[1] in which he forgives his future assassin, touched the hearts of many and this short document has already become a spiritual classic. Furthermore, his standing as a scholar and man of God has become more widely acknowledged following the publication of his homilies, talks and a few major papers on Christian–Muslim relations.

Father Christian was the only intellectual among the Tibhirine community and his commitment to dialogue with Islam was also perhaps more central to his monastic vocation than that of his fellow monks. In looking in previous chapters at the lives of Brs Jean-Pierre, Luc and Michel, we gained an insight into three of the four forms of dialogue as outlined by the Vatican document *Dialogue and Proclamation*, namely the dialogue of life or friendship, the dialogue of action and, to a lesser extent, the dialogue of religious experience. We meet the fourth form of dialogue, that of theological exchange, in the life and witness of Fr Christian.

As Fr Christian matured in his monastic vocation, he developed the capacity to understand and speak the language of the heart, an indispensable requirement for inter-religious dialogue. This spiritual development went hand in hand with

---

1. See Appendix 1.

his growing friendship with the Muslim villagers of Tibhirine and with his role as spiritual father to the monastic community. However, we need to remember that his devotion to dialogue wasn't primarily an intellectual pursuit but one which had its roots deeply embedded in his personal history, an existential commitment of the heart as much as of the head.

A COMMON ORIGIN AND A COMMON DESTINY

Father Christian was born to Guy and Monique de Chergé in Colmar, France, on 18 January 1937, the second of eight children. The de Chergé family were part of the *haute bourgeoisie Parisienne*, a family with a strong sense of duty and service. His father was from a military family and rose to the rank of general whereas on his mother's side there was a strong tradition of the religious life. Father Christian's father was posted to Algiers in 1942 and the family followed him there in October of that same year; he was five years old and was to remain in Algeria until May 1945. Like most Europeans in Algeria at this time he had little contact with the local Muslim population. However, he couldn't help but notice the fervour of their religious practice and their reverence in prayer. Whereas his brothers found it amusing to see people praying in the streets when the Mosque overflowed for Friday prayer, Christian was intrigued.

He was later to describe this as a pivotal moment in his understanding of Islam. 'It is now forty years this very year that for the first time I saw people praying in a different manner than my father's. I was five years old and I was discovering Algeria for a first stay of three years. I am still profoundly grateful to my mother who taught us, my brothers and me, to respect the uprightness and the attitudes embodied in this Muslim prayer. "They are praying to God," my mother used to say. Thus I always knew that the God of Islam and the God of Jesus Christ aren't different.'[2] This realisation that we have and worship the one God immediately gives Christians and Muslims a common origin and a common destiny, it makes us all sons and daughters of the one Father and thereby brothers and sisters. The enlightened approach of his mother had helped to free the young Christian from the sometimes hostile attitude of the Roman Catholic Church at that time towards other denominations and faiths.

A LADDER UNITING HEAVEN AND EARTH

In July 1959, Fr Christian, then a seminarian for the Archdiocese of Paris, had to interrupt his studies to do his military service in Algeria where the war of independence from France had been raging since 1 November 1954. He was assigned to the SAP, the Special Administrative Sections, whose mission it was to win over the local population to the French presence. His role was mainly administrative but it did also have a military component. Father Christian was fascinated by the religious devotion of the Muslim population and struck up a close friendship with an uneducated rural policeman, a devout Muslim and father of ten. Their regular discussions developed into a spiritual friendship. Then one day Mohammed had to intervene to protect Christian's life which had been threatened by the FLN, the National Liberation Front. The following day Mohammed paid with his own life for this courageous act of friendship; he was found assassinated by the edge of a well. This supreme act of love by a Muslim friend was to mark Fr Christian profoundly for the rest of his life. How could he forget the love shown to him by this simple and holy man? The repercussions of this event

---

2. Marie-Christine Ray, *Christian de Chergé, Prieur de Tibhirine* (Paris: Bayard Éditions/Centurion, 1998), pp. 20–1.

were to dictate the rest of Fr Christian's life, both his existential choices and his understanding of Islam. Mohammed's act of pure love revealed to Fr Christian the beauty of God's love at work in his Muslim brothers and sisters.

In a seminal article in *Islamochristiana*,[3] Fr Christian looks forward to the day when he will be reunited with Mohammed in the communion of saints:

> Since then it is my firm hope that I shall see in the communion of all the elect with Christ, this beloved brother who lived, even unto death the commandment of perfect love. This afterlife of the communion of saints, where Christians and Muslims, and so many others with them, share the same filial joy – it is up to us to show it visibly, like all the other mysteries of the Kingdom. And how should we go about it except by loving as of now, gratuitously, those whom a mysterious plan of God prepares and sanctifies by the way of Islam, and by living with them the Eucharistic sharing of the everyday?[4]

Here Fr Christian shares with us his 'firm hope' for complete communion and mutual recognition in love in the afterlife, a recognition that also implies a programme for action in this world, a sharing of the many values Christians and Muslims hold in common, 'the eucharistic sharing of the everyday'.

Ora et Labora, prayer and work, are the two traditional characteristics of the monastic life. And Fr Christian saw these also as the key to the existential dialogue that should characterise

---

3. *Islamochristiana*, 23 (1997), pp. 1–26, Pontificio Instituto Di Studi Arabi e D'Islamistica.
4. Ibid., p. 18.

the Christian community's encounter with Islam. Father Christian liked to use the image of the ladder uniting heaven and earth to describe this common journey. Both communities share a common origin and a common humanity and thus the ladder is firmly based on this shared human foundation. The two religions can be seen to represent the two sides of the ladder and the rungs joining the sides represent their shared endeavours to reach the ultimate communion of the saints in the afterlife.

COMMON SPIRITUAL PRACTICES

Father Christian was keen to highlight the common spiritual practices shared by both faiths. These commonalities include:

> the gift of the self to the Absolute of God, regular prayer, fasting, the sharing of almsgiving, the conversion of the heart, the constant remembering of the Presence which has a name (*dhikr,* ejaculatory prayer, the prayer of Jesus), trust in Providence, the necessity of hospitality which knows no frontiers, the call to spiritual struggle, pilgrimage which is also interior … In all that how can one not recognise the Spirit of Holiness, of which no one knows from where it comes nor where it goes (Jn 3:8), from where it comes down nor how it goes up[5]

Elsewhere Fr Christian draws our attention to the centrality of God's mercy in Muslim thinking, the root of the word mercy 'rhm' appearing up to three hundred and thirty-nine times in the Qur'an.[6] Mercy is also a quality Christians see as integral to

---

5. Ibid., p. 11.
6. Bruno Chenu, *L'invincible espérance* (Paris: Bayard Éditions/Centurion, 1997), p. 74.

their understanding of a God who is love (cf. 1 Jn 4:8). Father Christian recognises here not only the many common spiritual practices which Islam and Christianity share, inspired by the Holy Spirit, but also draws attention to the similarities between the monastic way of life and Islam.

Father Christian was drawn to the monastic way of life in a Muslim setting in order to give witness to the fact that Christians are also people of prayer. The monastic practice of gathering in church to pray seven times a day would be a powerful sign to the Muslim community which comes together five times a day to pray. He knew that this common devotion to prayer and worship, the acknowledgment of the divine transcendence, would be the strongest foundation for spiritual friendship and mutual encouragement. The memory of Mohammed's final words to him was a legacy and an inspiration: 'Knowing himself to be under threat, he [Mohammed] had accepted, among other kinds of support, that "I should pray for him". He had simply remarked "I know that you will pray for me. But, you know, Christians don't know how to pray!" I understood this comment as a reproach addressed to a Church which didn't appear, then, at least visibly, as a community of prayer.'[7]

The Gift of Difference

It's worth recalling that Fr Christian not only rejoiced in the common rungs of the mystical ladder which Christians and Muslims share but he also valued their differences as a reflection of the difference in unity of the three persons of the Trinity and also as a reflection of God's infinite creativity in creation, the scriptures and the human personality. Father Christian points out that both the Qur'an and the Bible extol

---

7. Ray, p. 48.

the variety and profusion of God's creativity. He writes: 'The refrain is often repeated [in the Qur'an]: difference is a "sign" for whoever knows how to see and wishes to be instructed. It is a language willed by the Creator on whom depends everything which differs.'[8] As St John Paul II said: 'There are undeniably differences that reflect the genius and the spiritual "riches" which God has given to the peoples' (cf. *Ad Gentes,* no. 11).[9] And, of course, there are differences too which, as the Pope goes on to point out, are due to 'the spirit of evil in history'.[10]

Thus, for Fr Christian, differences between Muslims and Christians aren't necessarily irreconcilable in the greatness of the completely Other who is God and in the communion of saints for which He is preparing us. God is always greater and beyond our understanding. In the great mystery of the Trinity we find that unity is achieved through the difference of relationship. 'God who is love is essentially a being of relationships. If we are allowed to have a mystique of difference, it's really because the latter originates in God himself. ... The Spirit alone can produce difference. He is the link par excellence. He guarantees personally the perfect union while safeguarding the Persons; a fusion without confusion.'[11]

Saint John Paul II, speaking about dialogue with Islam, explained the difference within the oneness of the Trinity as follows: 'Each [person] possesses the divine substance whole and indivisible, but each is distinct from the other by virtue of their reciprocal relations.'[12] And the Qur'an states that our

---

8. Chenu, p. 120.
9. Saint John Paul II's Christmas Address to the Roman Curia, 22 December 1986, www.ewtn.com
10. Ibid.
11. Chenu, p. 158.
12. Saint John Paul 11, General Audience, 5 May 1999, *Muslims and Christians Adore the One God,* www.ewtn.com

different faiths are according to God's plan for humankind and that God will clarify these issues for us in the afterlife. In the meantime we should try to outdo each other in good deeds: 'If God had pleased He could surely have made you one people (professing one faith). But He wished to try and test you by that which He gave you. So try to excel in good deeds. To Him will you all return in the end, when He will tell you of what you were at variance' (5:48).[13]

STUMBLING BLOCKS

Father Christian goes on to say in the same article that the two great stumbling blocks in Christianity for Muslims are our conception of the three persons of the Trinity and our affirmation of the crucifixion of Jesus as the summit of his redemptive incarnation. Whereas for Christians the stumbling blocks in Islam are the mission of the prophet Mohammed and the place of the Qur'an in divine revelation. The union between Christian and Muslim that will be attained in the communion of saints, says Fr Christian, must be begun by 'the quasi-sacrament of a trusting understanding between us as from now'.[14] As part of this 'quasi-sacrament', he nourished himself by meditating on the Qur'an (in addition, of course, to his pondering of the Christian scriptures). Christian had no doubt that God's spirit could speak to him through the Qur'an if he was willing to approach it in a spirit of humility and openness. He writes: 'It has often happened to me that I've seen suddenly emerge from the Qur'an, in the course of a reading which was at first difficult and disconcerting, a condensed version of the Gospel which then becomes a true

13. Jaroslav Pelikan, ed., *Sacred Writings, Volume 3 Islam: The Qur'an* (Karachi: Quality Paperback Book Club, 1992), p. 104.
14. Chenu, p. 164.

way of communion with the other and with God.'[15]

And, of course, the real agent of fruitful difference and genuine unity is the Holy Spirit. Father Christian summed this up beautifully in his spiritual testament when he wrote: 'My death will of course prove right those who have dismissed me as naïve or idealistic: "Let him tell us now what he thinks about it!" But those people must know that at last my most burning curiosity will be satisfied. I'll now be able, should it please God, to become absorbed in God's gaze in order to contemplate with him his children of Islam as he sees them, completely illuminated by Christ's glory, fruit of his Passion, filled by the gift of the Spirit whose secret joy it will always be to establish communion and to re-establish likeness, while playfully enjoying the differences.'[16]

Everything is Simple when God is in Control

Father Christian and the monks of Tibhirine liked to describe themselves as people of prayer alongside a people of prayer. The witness of the monastic community didn't need to be explained to their Muslim neighbours. They could see them praying seven times a day, more often even than themselves. The monks were outdoing them in spiritual fervour, a form of spiritual emulation recommended by the Qur'an (5:2). The work of the Holy Spirit in bringing about greater understanding and unity between Christian and Muslim is at its most powerful in the realm of prayer where dogmatic barriers are side-stepped and people open themselves to the unifying action of the Spirit.

As St John Paul II stated, true prayer is always the work of the Holy Spirit. 'We can indeed maintain that every authentic prayer is called forth by the Holy Spirit, who is mysteriously

---

15. Ibid., p. 178.
16. See Appendix 1.

present in the heart of every person.'[17] So where there is true prayer the spirit of unity will flourish and bear fruit in a deeper realisation of our common sonship and common destiny. It is the work of the Spirit always to promote unity, a unity that is the fruit of love. Father Christian's vocation to a closer union with Islam through the monastic witness of a praying community was confirmed a year before his final vows in an unforgettable experience on the night of Sunday, 21 September 1975.

Father Christian returned to the chapel after Compline and prostrated himself in prayer between the altar and the tabernacle. Suddenly he became aware of another presence beside the altar, also prostrated in prayer. The man, who was a Muslim guest in the monastery and scarcely known to Christian, began to pray aloud, praising God from the depths of his being. This was followed by a silence and the guest turned towards Fr Christian, 'Pray for me.' They were later joined by a third person, a priest, Lucien Rivaud, who was spending a sabbatical year in the monastery. The symphony of prayer was further amplified 'in the fusion of these three different expressions of a single and same fidelity, that of the Spirit who is in God, who says God'. The prayer, which actually started at 8 p.m. and concluded after 11. p.m, had passed by as if in a single instant. Father Christian never again met this 'friend of a single night' apart from the following day when all he said to Christian was, 'Everything is simple when God is in control.'[18]

Through the purifying fire of the Holy Spirit two Christians and a Muslim were united in several hours of intense prayer breaking down, through the power of love, the centuries old

---

17. Pope John Paul II's Christmas Address to Roman Curia, 22 December 1986.
18. The account of this 'Night of Fire' is in Chenu, pp. 33–8.

barriers of fear and mistrust. The Muslim guest commented that despite his fear of joining Fr Christian in prayer 'it was as if there was a power within him which impelled him' and Christian wondered 'if God himself were laughing at the amusing joke which he had just played on centuries of mutual cursing among brothers called to pray to Him'. This 'night of fire' confirmed Fr Christian in his monastic vocation to a Muslim people.

A Lifelong Commitment

Before his solemn profession on 1 October 1976 – the feast of St Thérèse of Lisieux, the patroness of missionaries – Christian had spent two years, starting in August 1972, studying Islam and Arabic with the White Fathers in Rome. This meant that he was the sole member of the community to have an academic grounding in Islam. While all the members of the community wished to serve the people of Algeria and engage in a dialogue of friendship and everyday life, they were uncertain about how far the community should go in the domain of spiritual sharing. They were aware of being a tiny island in the vast ocean of Islam and were understandably worried about weakening their Christian and monastic identity.

Father Jean-Pierre, one of the two survivors of the Tibhirine community, had this to say: 'Thus, for example, an unbalanced devotion to the oneness of God could lead imperceptibly to the downgrading of the divinity of Christ and of his central place in the spiritual life. One could also end up, through a well-intentioned sympathy for the other culture, by putting Holy Scripture on an equal footing with the texts of Islam even in the liturgy or in personal meditation.'[19] Father Christian, on

19. In an interview given to me in French at Midelt, Morocco, in July 2007.

the other hand, was fired by a vision of our common humanity and spiritual destiny, and of the potential for growing in unity which the presence of the Holy Spirit, also active in Islam (*SEE NOSTRA AETATE*, para., 2), gives to both communities.

Before his final vows Fr Christian submitted to the community a reflection on the step he was about to take, a document entitled *The Meaning of a Call*.[20] It is divided into eight unequal sections each of which starts with 'I profess a call ...'. Its language is heavily redolent of the Qur'an and of monastic literature, in equal measure. He stresses the importance of submission to God's will and of openness to God's Word. This *lectio divina* (the prayerful pondering of scripture in the context of one's daily life) of the Christian scriptures, of nature and of the human heart, he writes, calls for a prayerful listening to the voice of God in all of these medias, including a listening to the Book of Islam.

THE RIBÂT ES-SALAM: A DEEPER SPIRITUAL COMMUNION

A few years after his solemn vows, Fr Christian found an outlet for his desire to enter into a deeper spiritual communion with Islam. In 1979 Fr Christian and Claude Rault[21] founded *The Ribât es-Salam, The Bond of Peace*, a Christian group which met for two days twice a year at the monastery of Tibhirine in order to develop a deeper understanding of, and stronger spiritual links with, the Muslim community. While shopping in nearby Médéa, one of the Tibhirine monks, Fr Jean-Pierre, met a Sufi, or practitioner of the mystical dimension in Islam, who expressed a desire to get to know the monks. Out of this chance encounter a group of

---

20. This document is reproduced in Ray, pp. 110–14.
21. A White Father and currently Bishop of the Diocese of Laghouat-Ghardaïa in the Sahara.

Sufis joined the *Ribât* for its meetings at Tibhirine. They weren't interested in dogmatic discussions but in journeying together in prayer. The meetings involved an exchange on a theme, proposed alternately by each group, and of a time of prayer.

The functioning and purpose of this group of spiritual sharing was beautifully explained to me by Fr Jean-Pierre:

> From the first meetings the Muslim Sufis insisted that dogmatic questions should not be tackled because they lead to division. Rather one had to aim at what unites in the truth. It was to convert ourselves by our 'submission' to God. Note that we are here in the train of thought of the Prologue to the Rule of St Benedict with its insistence on 'listening' and the conversion of the heart. The word 'Islam' means 'submission'. They say that there was an 'Islam' before 'Islam', citing the case of Abraham, the model of those who are submitted to God. There can therefore be an 'Islam' outside of Islam. Thus Fr Christian in that same sense used to say that the most perfect of the 'submitted' was Jesus. The type of 'conversion' here proposed seems to bring us to the heart of the charism of Fr Christian as regards Islam, a submission to God, to be sought together.

> Two means were employed: silent prayer and *dhikr*. This wasn't a question of ritual prayer, whether it be Muslim or Christian but a praying together in silence. To remain silent together to 'listen' to God, what God has to say. To succeed in doing this during a meeting unites the participants very deeply. They discover each other as children of God, together under his gaze, although different; loved by him together. God through his Spirit makes links that are surprising, astonishing, respectful, welcoming, and friendly;

people perceive themselves to be children of the same God, brothers and sisters.

The *dhikr*[22] is a word drawn from one or the other tradition [i.e. Catholic or Muslim], a word to be chewed by each one in private, to be listened to, meditated in their heart, a word destined to be lived; in this way one submits to God, one obeys Him. Such a word is adopted by common agreement and then lived as an act of submission to the Spirit of God who acts in us, and this practice of attentiveness and obedience for a period of time converts us by drawing us closer to each other. It makes us similar to each other by conforming us to a common wish of the Lord. It creates links, links of brotherhood in the name of the one living God. Following on from this time of listening and living in the light of this word, there was a sharing of what had been lived at the next meeting. The grace was pooled.[23]

Father Christian would write about these encounters: 'There is a fraternal listening to Islam which can bring us back to the very heart of the mystery of God, in a humble attachment to a Christ always greater than anything we can say or show in our lives of him.'[24] Through his membership of *The Bond of Peace* Christian was given the gift of a deeper spiritual communion with the heart of Islam.

---

22. *Dhikr* is defined by Jo O'Donovan, as 'the prayer of remembrance, in which the mind is centred by the repetition of the Divine Names on the beads, or by the recital of short verses from the Qur'an', *Understanding Differently Christianity and the World Religions* (Veritas Publications, Dublin, 2012), p. 151.
23. In an interview given to me in French at Midelt, Morocco, in July 2007.
24. Marie-Christine Ray, *Christian De Chergé prieur de Tibhirine* (Paris: Bayard Éditions/Centurion, 1998), p. 148.

THE GUARDIAN OF MY BROTHER

With the assassination, just five kilometres from the monastery, of the twelve Croatian construction workers in December 1993, Christian and the other monks sensed that the noose was tightening about them. These workers, personally known to the monks, had had their throats cut for the sole reason that they were Christians. The leader of the hit group was the notorious emir Sayah Attia renowned for his brutality and reputed to have cut the throats of one hundred and forty-five people. The local press referred to him as a 'filthy beast'. When Sayah and a small band of five men invaded the monastery on Christmas Eve 1993 the monks thought that the end had come. Sayah demanded to see the 'pope', Fr Christian. In an encounter lasting a quarter of an hour he made the following demands of Christian: that Fr Luc, the monk doctor, should travel to tend to their wounded, and that money and medical supplies be donated.

Father Christian courageously refused his demands while at the same time explaining that he had no objections to any sick person being attended to at Br Luc's dispensary. When told by Sayah that he had no choice, Fr Christian replied that he had. He then went on to tell the intruder that they were preparing to celebrate the feast of the Prince of Peace and Sayah had entered the monastery armed. Sayah Attia appeared touched by this remark and replied: 'Excuse me, I didn't know.' After shaking the hands of the monks present he departed, promising to return. And life returned to 'normal' for the monks who set about getting ready for the Christmas Vigil and Midnight Mass.

In his encounter with Sayah, Fr Christian showed his true spiritual mettle. Faced with imminent death he refused to be intimidated but even more impressively he refused to see the 'beast' in Sayah but tried to glimpse instead the image and likeness of God. Father Christian later wrote that he had stood up to Sayah 'not only because I was the guardian of my brothers, but also because in fact I was also the guardian of this brother who was there before me and who ought to be able to discover in himself something other than that which he had become. And that's more or less what happened to the extent that he gave way, that he made an effort to understand.'[25] As regards judging him, Fr Christian has this to say: 'Each one of his crimes is terrible, but he isn't a filthy beast. It's now up to the mercy of God to show itself.'[26] Father Christian's prayer for Sayah and for his companions was that they be disarmed, turned away from violence. But he also made this prayer for himself and for his community, that they too would enter upon the path of forgiveness and non-violence. In this encounter, and Christian's subsequent reactions, we can see his spiritual greatness, the greatness of someone who had truly absorbed Jesus' Sermon on the Mount and who lived it out without compromise. Of course, the prudent men of our generation would describe his action as folly. And that is exactly what it was, the folly of the cross.

UNITED IN THE COMMUNION OF SAINTS

Father Christian was not a systematic theologian, someone who sought to work out a rigorous approach to Islam in the comfort of his study. His theology sprang from his encounter with individual Muslims and the Muslim community in Algeria. That a Muslim had given his life for him had a profound impact upon him. The 'greater love' of this uneducated father of ten had shown him with absolute certainty that God's love, God's Holy Spirit, was alive

---

25. Chenu, pp. 309–10.
26. Ibid., p. 310.

and active in the devout followers of Islam. He could not doubt that his friend Mohammed was in heaven, in the communion of saints, united with all the countless saints who had followed a path of submission to God's loving will for their lives.

Christian Salenson, in his painstaking and excellent book on Fr Christian's theology,[27] stresses the key role which eschatology plays in the latter's understanding of Islam. He sees him as starting from this rock of certainty, namely, that Mohammed is now in the communion of saints, in God's presence, praising and worshipping Him for all eternity. And from this premise he tries to work out his understanding of the place of Islam in God's plan of salvation. No doubt this insight is true but I doubt if it had in practice a determining influence on his understanding of Islam. It seems to me that Fr Christian's living of the monastic life, with its similarities in practice to Islam and the role of the Holy Spirit, are more important. Eschatology gives us a common destiny and, of course, we all have a common origin in the Fatherhood of God but neither insight is of much help in discerning how we should relate to each other in everyday life as we search for God.

Father Christian himself says as much when he writes that the communion of saints is a 'mystery, essential for us, which indicates the place of encounter without clarifying how to get there. By allowing ourselves to be moved, the Spirit of Jesus is free to do his work among us making use of difference, even of what disturbs us. We recognise him at his work. We experience in silent prayer lived out side by side over a long period, in particular with our Sufi friends, a feeling of fullness which is all

---

27. Christian Salenson, *Christian de Chergé, une théologie de l'espérance*, Paris: Bayard, 2009; translated into English as *Christian de Chergé, A Theology of Hope* (Collegeville, MN: Liturgical Press, 2012).

the more real as we know it to be deeply shared. "God knows more about it!"[28]

THE HOLY SPIRIT: GOD'S BOND OF UNITY AND LOVE

A theology of the Holy Spirit is required to ground these insights and this is exactly what was provided by the Second Vatican Council. 'All this [the hope of the resurrection] holds true not only for Christians but also for all people of good will in whose hearts grace is active invisibly. For since Christ died for everyone, and since all are in fact called to one and the same destiny, which is divine, we must hold that the Holy Spirit offers to all the possibility of being made partners, in a way known to God, in the paschal mystery.'[29] Once you accept that the Holy Spirit, the Spirit sent by the Father and Jesus, is operative in Muslims and that it's possible for 'a ray of the truth' (*Nostra Aetate*, 2) to be found in the Qur'an, and 'seeds of the Word … hidden among them' (*Ad Gentes*, 11), then you throw wide open the doors to greater cooperation at the communal and spiritual level.

Our common humanity and origin provide a good foundation for the dialogue of everyday life through friendship and the promotion of human values in society but, as Fr Christian realises, the greater and deeper unity comes about through recognising the purifying action of the Holy Spirit, God's bond of unity and love, at work in both religious communities. In a retreat preached to the Little Sisters of Jesus in Morocco in November 1990 Fr Christian said: 'I can

---

28. Bruno Chenu, ed. *Sept vies pour Dieu et l'Algérie* (Paris: Bayard Éditions/Centurion, 1996), p. 72.
29. Austin Flannery OP, General Editor, *The Basic Sixteen Documents, Vatican Council 11, Gaudium et Spes*, 22 (Dublin: Dominican Publications, 1996) p. 186.

go to encounter the other because the life of the Spirit dwells also in the other and, although I know this, it will always be a disconcerting experience for all apostles of every age to make the same discovery as Peter made in his encounter with Cornelius and his household: "God gave them the same gift that he gave us! (Acts 11:17)."[30]

GOD'S WELL

Some may wonder if a concern for the truth of Christian revelation has been pushed to one side in an effort to erase differences in our understanding of the ways of God. In fact some Islamologists[31] might find Fr Christian's approach naïve, especially his esteem for the Qur'an and his use of it for *lectio divina*. They would pose the question: How can a book which rejects the central truths of Christian revelation, the trinity and the incarnation, be inspired by the Holy Spirit? Father Christian, however, did not see his spiritual affinity with, and love of, his Muslim brothers and sisters as being anything other than a search for the truth, a truth which is always greater and beyond anything we can encapsulate in our limited human understanding of the mystery of God.

He wrote: 'For, just as the love of a brother proclaims the truth of our love for God, likewise our willingness to recognise and welcome the fragment of truth deposited in the heart of a brother will express, better than any other discourse, our thirst

---

30. Salenson, p. 193.

31. In his book, *La Bible Face Au Coran* (Paris: L'oeuvre Éditions, 2011), the French theologian and Islamologist, Fr François Jourdan, is highly critical of the naïveté of Christian Islamologists who fail to appreciate the radical difference between the Christian understanding of God as revealed in the two Testaments and the understanding of God to be found in the Qur'an.

and our love of Truth which is only in God. Those who thus try to grow in mutual love cannot but progress together towards the Truth which surpasses them and unites them forever.'[32] In short we need the insights, example and love of others, of different religions or of none, if we're to grow more and more into the Truth found fully in God alone.

As Fr Christian's theology is existential, based on his experience of living with Muslims and of living the monastic life, I have tried to focus in this chapter on significant encounters and moments of insight in his life. The following well-known encounter could be said to epitomise Fr Christian's relationship with his many Muslim friends. A young Muslim man in the neighbourhood, M., had asked Fr Christian out of the blue to teach him how to pray. One day M. reminded his instructor that it had been a long time since they 'had dug their well together', a long time since they had last had a spiritual conversation. In a teasing manner Fr Christian asked him, 'And at the bottom of our well, what will we find? Muslim water or Christian water?' M. looked at Christian bemusedly, 'All the same, we've been journeying together for such a long time, and you're still asking yourself that question! … You know, at the bottom of that particular well, what one finds is God's water!'[33] And having found that water we will discover, Christian and Muslim, that it is a spring, deep within us, welling up to eternal life.

---

32. 'Prier en Église à l'Écoute de l'Islam', *Chemins de Dialogue*, 27 (2006), p. 23.

33. *Islamochristiana*, 23 (1997), pp. 15–16.

PART 2

The Algerian Church:
The Gift of Encounter

CHAPTER SIX

Learning to Love Our Muslim Neighbours

In the second half of this book I look at the relationship between the tiny Catholic Church in Algeria and the overwhelmingly Muslim population. The many stories of encounter I relate are taken from the life of this small, though vibrant, Church community. These stories are a wonderful example of how the Gospel message can speak beyond the boundaries of the Christian Church and become a ferment of communion between Muslims and Christians. But also, perhaps more importantly, the Algerian Church can teach us in the West how to respond to Islam, how to see the face of Christ in our Muslim neighbour. What is striking about the witness of this tiny Christian remnant is that it is willing not only to give but also to receive God's love from its Muslim neighbours. The realisation that our Muslim brothers and sisters are truly sons and daughters of the one God offers the Christian Church a way to reimagine its relationship with Islam. Instead of viewing Islam as a threat, it can begin to work towards cultivating a spirit of mutual esteem, seeing moderate Muslims as fellow believers in the one God and partners in bringing in God's Kingdom.

PARTNERS IN BRINGING IN GOD'S KINGDOM

The plight of the tiny Christian community in Algeria came to the attention of the English-speaking world with the assassination of the seven Cistercian monks of Tibhirine in 1996 and of Pierre Claverie, the Bishop of Oran, shortly afterwards.

It was only in January 1997 that I became aware of this crisis afflicting the Algerian Church and people. On 12 January 1997 *The Tablet* carried an interview with Mgr Teissier, Archbishop of Algiers, which deeply impressed me. I sensed something of his love for the Algerian people and his conviction that the Gospel was truly Good News, something of ultimate importance. The journalist wrote that he 'was moved by [his] visit to a priest of such dedication and fortitude'. His courage and desire to stay alongside the Algerian people in their hour of need touched me. I then forgot about the article absorbed by the demands of daily life.

A few months later I referred to Mgr Teissier's courageous witness in a homily at Mass, comparing his willingness to risk his life for his flock to Jesus' sacrificial act of love for us in the Eucharist. Shortly afterwards I suddenly felt inspired to write to Archbishop Teissier to offer a word of support. I didn't have his address and just sent my short letter to the Archevêque d'Alger, Alger, Algeria, and promptly forgot all about it. To my surprise a few months later a reply arrived, written on behalf of the Archbishop by Fr John MacWilliam, a former student of Worth School where I was chaplain. I didn't know that Fr John was in Algeria so this added another twist, so to speak, to the plot. That surprising turn of events eventually led to the first of my two visits to Algeria and subsequently to the writing of a book, *Christian Martyrs for a Muslim People*,[1] recounting the witness of the nineteen martyrs and the life of the Church which had produced them.

Monsignor Henri Teissier, Archbishop Emeritus of Algiers, has, in the footsteps of the great Cardinal Duval, his predecessor,

---

1. Martin McGee OSB, *Christian Martyrs for a Muslim People* (New York/Mahwah NJ: Paulist Press, 2008).

been an indefatigable advocate of the value of Christian–Muslim encounter. He writes:

> The life of the Church in Algeria offers an opportunity to begin a new era of mission, that of giving Christian witness to believers who belong to another religion. This is not a matter of denying the possibility of Muslim conversions to Christianity. Moreover they exist today more than in the past. It is a question more of trying to discover how God's gift to us through the life of Christ can also become a sign for non-Christians, in this case for Muslims. Moreover, this movement is reciprocal because we have also to discover the faithfulness of our Muslim brothers to the call which God addresses to them, deep within their conscience, and to accept their witness as a support for our own faithfulness to God.[2]

In other words, Christians and Muslims can become partners in bringing in God's Kingdom, if they can only learn to be attentive and responsive to the gift of God, God's Holy Spirit, at work in each other.

THE 'THREE DEATHS' OF THE ALGERIAN CHURCH
In his book *Chrétiens En Algérie: Un Partage D'Espérance*[3] Mgr Henri Teissier reflected on the 'three deaths' of the Catholic

---

2. Henri Teissier, 'A new season for the Church of Algeria', *Oasis*, 2 September 2005, online since 12 May 2009.
3. Henri Teissier, *Chrétiens En Algérie: Un Partage D'Espérance* (Christians in Algeria: A Sharing of Hope) (Paris: Desclée de Brouwer, 2002).

Church in Algeria.[4] Firstly, there was the mass exodus in 1962 of eight hundred thousand European settlers after the country gained its independence. Secondly, in 1976 Church schools and hospitals were nationalised as part of a general nationalisation programme undertaken by the socialist government. The third 'death' occurred between 1993 and 1996 when the GIA (Armed Islamic Group) issued its ultimatum to all foreigners to leave the country by 1 December 1993 or face execution. Many priests and religious left, as well as most of the remaining foreign Christian families and native Algerian Catholics, but many religious and priests also stayed on out of solidarity with the suffering Algerian people. Between 1994 and 1996 nineteen priests and religious were assassinated. Among the most prominent victims of the Islamists were Mgr Pierre Claverie OP, Bishop of Oran, and the seven Cistercian monks of Tibhirine.

At the end of this third 'death' of the Church, there remains a tiny remnant of about three thousand laity and three hundred priests, religious and lay assistants. The Catholic community has now been reduced to a shadow of its former self but has retained its four dioceses: the Archdiocese of Algiers, and the Dioceses of Oran, Constantine and Hippo, and Laghouat-Ghardaïa (also known as the Diocese of the Sahara). In 1962, before independence, it had approximately one million members,

---

4. There were Christian communities in North Africa from the second century onwards. In the fifth century it had up to six hundred bishoprics, the most famous of its bishops being St Augustine of Hippo (modern-day Annaba in Algeria) and St Cyprian of Carthage. However successive Arab/Muslim invasions between the seventh and twelfth century succeeded in wiping out the Christian Church. With the landing of the French forces at Sidi-Ferruch in 1830, a new era in the life of the Church began, namely that of a colonial presence made up of European settlers from France, Spain, Italy and Malta.

many of whom would, of course, have been non-practising. At present the majority of Church members are Catholic students from sub-Saharan Africa who are studying in Algeria on bursaries given by the Algerian government. Then there are women married to Algerian Muslims, foreign workers in the oil fields and construction industry and a growing number of African migrants hoping to make their way to Europe. Finally there are a small number of *pieds-noirs*, Europeans born in Algeria who stayed on after independence, and a small but growing number of Algerian converts.

A BRUTAL CIVIL WAR

In 1992 a brutal civil war broke out in Algeria between Islamic fundamentalists and a military-dominated government. The civil war was fuelled by both social and religious discontent. In the 1980s a high youth unemployment rate, a fall in the price of oil, the corruption which inevitably flows from a one-party state and a rapidly growing population, all fed into the unrest which was to explode onto the streets in 1988. In addition, these social conditions gave an added impetus to the rise of a fundamentalist reading of Islam, which saw itself as the only force capable of opposing successfully the ambient social corruption. This fundamentalism, which sought to return to the pure teaching of the Qur'an and the tradition of the Prophet Mohammed, made its way into Algeria from the Muslim Brotherhood in Egypt and the Wahabite Islam of Saudia Arabia. As well as affecting negatively the role of women in society and the dress code, the rise of Islamism also encouraged some Muslims to regard their Christian neighbours with suspicion.

Fearful of a victory by the Islamic Salvation Front in the second round of the general election in 1992, the army cancelled the ballot, thereby unleashing a bloody civil war. An estimated one hundred thousand to one hundred and fifty thousand people lost their lives during the height of the violence, the 'black decade' of 1992 to 2002. And the tiny Christian community also bore its share of the bloodshed. Between 1994 and 1996 about one hundred Christians were murdered. Included among this number were the nineteen priests and religious assassinated in cold blood as they went about their daily work of serving the poorest sections of Algerian society.

With the gradual reduction in the level of violence from 1998 onwards, the Church had begun to hope that life would gradually return to normal. Alas these hopes were not fully realised. Firstly, the violence returned to the streets of Algiers in 2007 with suicide bombers and car bombings causing many civilian victims. However, since then violent terrorist attacks have almost completely ceased, with the exception of the attack on the In Amenas gas plant on 16 January 2013 which killed forty people. The second major setback in recent years has been the government's crackdown on evangelical Christians and, to everybody's surprise, the Catholic Church has also been targeted. So why, one may wonder, has this unexpected change of attitude, on the part of the Algerian government towards the Christian community, come about? The hostile criticism in the media, especially in the Arab-language press, of the increasing number of evangelical converts appears to have provoked a panicked reaction on the part of the government. This reaction is undoubtedly related to a desire by the government not to offend the Islamists as part of their effort to restore peace.

Evangelical Converts

The growth of evangelical churches, especially in Kabylia, drew the attention of the press with many sensational stories and some reports going so far as to claim that up to fifty per cent of Kabylia was now Christian. This in turn led to the decree of 28 February 2006 which sought to regulate the practice of non-Muslim worship and punish any attempt by the evangelicals to proselytise. Worship can now only take place in church buildings recognised as such by the civil authorities. This means that Mass can no longer be celebrated legally in the open air or in buildings other than churches. This considerably restricts the work of the Church in the university towns and industrial sites that have no legally recognised place of worship.

Thus on 30 January 2008, Fr Pierre Wallez, a priest of the diocese of Oran, was given a two-year suspended sentence and a hefty fine for praying with Christian sub-Saharan migrants outside a recognised place of worship. According to this ruling the only place permissible for Christian prayer would be inside an authorised church. The sentence was appealed by the Church and commuted to a two-month suspended sentence and the fine was also reduced. Evangelical converts in Tiaret were sentenced to imprisonment for allegedly attending a 'Mass' in a private home, another evangelical woman was tried for possessing ten Bibles, and Dr Hugh Johnson, a retired pastor and former president of the Algerian Protestant Church, was refused permission to continue residing in Algeria despite forty-five years of residency. Catholic priests have been stopped by the police and accused of proselytism on the basis of carrying their Bible and breviary; and the Church has also had to struggle with an administration reluctant to grant visas for new religious or lay volunteers. However, over the last few years, in the face of Church protest and international publicity, this harassment of Christians appears to have subsided, for the moment at least.

The estimated number of evangelical converts since the 1980s varies wildly. Mustapha Krim, the Algerian President of the Algerian Protestant Church (EPA), in a recent article for the

Algerian Catholic Church magazine, *Pax & Concordia*,[5] stated that they had twenty-eight affiliated congregations and many sympathisers scattered throughout the country. As regards numbers he wrote: 'There don't exist any official statistics but we can reasonably accept the figure of thirty thousand of whom more than half have been baptised.' Many of the evangelical churches have now been closed down and await official registration as places of worship, a wait that, I suspect, will last indefinitely.

However, one encouraging sign in the midst of these troubles has been the growing support for the beleaguered Christian community by many Algerians. A petition, organised by the daily newspaper *El Watan* (26 May 2008) in favour of freedom of the press, trade unions and the Christian community, gathered about two thousand eight hundred signatures. Monsignor Teissier commented in the June edition of his diocesan magazine *Rencontres*, June 2008: 'Thus our trials have aroused the conscience of many people of Muslim origin.'

A Climate of Suspicion

In a lecture given on 30 October 2008 at Heythrop College, University of London, Mgr Teisiser pointed out that:

> the most destructive part of this campaign [of the mainly Arabic language press against the Christian presence in Algeria] has been the diffusion, through the mass media, of the idea that Christians are in Algeria exclusively for purposes of evangelisation. Insistence on this idea has given rise to a lack of confidence in Islamo–Christian relationships, particularly among ordinary people and traditional Islamic

---

5. *Revue de l'Église catholique d'Algérie*, 14 (2013), p. 20.

groups. Muslims who were in the habit, for years on end, of establishing relationships of mutual openness and trust and, indeed, of friendship with their Christian neighbours, have allowed themselves to become a prey to suspicion. Can you really trust a Christian? Doesn't he or she always have a secret agenda aimed at alienating us – both me and my children, whom he helps with their homework – from our fundamental beliefs as Muslims; and the discussion continues.[6]

Needless to say this climate of suspicion has made the mainly humanitarian and cultural work of the Church – such as the student libraries, Caritas, women's support groups and homework support – more problematic and precarious. The Catholic Church has made no attempt, unlike the evangelicals, to proselytize and is understandably upset at being subjected to the same harsh treatment as they. Monsignor Teissier, retired since 2008, and the current Archbishop of Algiers, a Jordanian, Monsignor Galeb Bader, and the other three Algerian bishops have always sought to work alongside the Algerian people as a leaven to bring about the coming of the Kingdom.

A Happy Surprise

The Catholic Church in Algeria had been marked by the legacy of Blessed Charles de Foucauld who sought to become the universal brother of the Muslims among whom he lived and died in Algeria in the early twentieth century. Now greatly reduced in number, the question of justifying her continued presence in this overwhelmingly Muslim country is never far from the

---

6. Lecture given by Mgr Teissier on 30 October 2008 at Heythrop College, University of London.

minds of the remaining faithful. Cardinal Duval, the leader of the Catholic Church in Algeria during and following the War of Independence, had intuited as early as 1956 the ground-breaking teaching of Vatican II that there were elements of truth and holiness in other non-Christian faiths and that every human being was in some mysterious way united to Christ in his paschal mystery. In his radio broadcast for Pentecost 1956, he stated that the Holy Spirit 'is sent even outside the visible Church to all people of goodwill'.[7] He pointed out that in dialogue with people of other faiths, or of none, God may be speaking through them to remind us of Gospel truths. The presence of the Spirit in all human relationships is the key insight that underpins the Church's continued presence in North Africa. What is new in this approach is the insight that in everyday encounters the Holy Spirit is also active in the Muslim partner, bringing God's grace and love to the Christian other; in other words the encounter is a two-way process of conversion. These daily relationships between Muslims and Christians are what the Algerian Church calls 'the sacrament of encounter',[8] outward signs of the transforming power of the Spirit.

The bishops don't see the role of the Church as being that of a chaplaincy to diplomats and other non-Algerians. It is rather a Church at the service of the Algerian people through its student libraries, literacy and women support groups and other social projects, a Church of encounter where the Holy Spirit is active in people of goodwill, whether they be Christian or Muslim,

---

7. Marie-Christine Ray, *Le Cardinal DUVAL* (Paris: Les Editions du Cerf, 1998), p. 81.
8. A fuller explanation of 'the sacrament of encounter' can be found in my book, Martin McGee OSB, *Christian Martyrs for a Muslim People* (New York/Mahwah NJ: Paulist Press, 2008), pp. 117–27.

bringing in the Kingdom. In a key document published in September 1979, the North African bishops wrote: 'The reign of God comes more fully through the knowledge of the mystery of Christ; it is already being fulfilled by the inauguration of the values of justice, truth, freedom, peace and love which are the fruits of the Spirit of God in all human relationships, at the heart of every person as within societal relationships themselves.'[9]

The Catholic Church has rightly sought to distance herself from the proselytising activities of some of the evangelicals. At the same time, however, the Church has to be seen to oppose the present efforts of the government to check the right of Algerians to openly practise as Christians or to become Christian. And, indeed, the Algerian Constitution does recognise the inviolable right of conscience and freedom of religious affiliation. It is in this difficult and challenging situation that the small but committed Catholic Church has sought to serve its Muslim neighbours and remain faithful to the Gospel. Great perseverance and courage have been required. But, above all, a humble love has been called for, in Mgr Teissier's words, 'un partage d'humanité', a sharing of a common humanity and a willingness to see the Holy Spirit at work in each other.

---

9. *Chrétiens au Maghreb – Le Sens de nos Rencontres*, Christians in the Maghreb – The Meaning of our Encounters (Documentation Catholique, 1979), pp. 1032–44.

CHAPTER SEVEN
Gospel Encounters

Reading the four diocesan magazines of the Algerian Church I have been struck by stories of encounter between Muslims and Christians which bring hope: hope to those involved in the encounters, hope to the Church in Algeria and also hope to those of us who may have contact with people of other faiths. The Algerian Church calls these meetings 'sacraments of encounter' (*sacrements de la rencontre*), moments when the individuals concerned experience God's presence and love through each other. In a recent pastoral letter to his diocese, Mgr Paul Desfarges, Bishop of Constantine and Hippo, described such an encounter as follows: 'To go to encounter someone is to open oneself to the mystery which they bear, to the unique way in which they embody it in their lives, beyond whatever can sometimes veil it and even smother it. That's why every true encounter is a happy surprise. It is a light on the presence of the Totally Other, in each other.'[1]

These sacraments of encounter are seen in the Gospels on the many occasions when Jesus brings God's healing love and presence into people's lives, both Jews and Gentiles. In chapter four of St John's Gospel, for example, Jesus tells the Samaritan woman at the well that he can give her 'the gift of God', living water welling up within her which leads to eternal life. In the sacrament of encounter, Christian and Muslim offer each other just such a gift when they enable each other to make contact with God's living presence in the other. It is such sacraments of encounter that offer

1. Mgr Paul Desfarges, *Une Église dans la Mangeoire* (A Church in the Manger), Christmas 2012, p. 7.

hope to the Algerian Church, signs of hope and signs of God's presence in the midst of its many trials and joys.

You Were a Stranger

On 12 February 2009 a new Bishop of Constantine and Hippo, Mgr Paul Desfarges SJ, a successor to the great St Augustine, was consecrated in the Basilica of Notre Dame d'Afrique in Algiers. Father Paul, a Frenchman, has lived for over thirty years in Algeria, taken out Algerian citizenship, and speaks fluent Arabic. He taught psychology for many years at the University of Constantine while at the same time acting as Vicar General of the diocese. As bishop with just about fifteen priests and a small number of religious he faces many challenges in his far-flung diocese, which has perhaps a thousand Christians, comprising for the most part African students studying at Algerian universities.

Lokmane Benchikh, a long-standing Muslim friend, welcomed Paul on behalf of the Muslims present at the ordination ceremony. Whether Lokmane realised it or not, his words strongly echoed chapter twenty-five of Matthew's Gospel where Jesus reminds us that in welcoming the marginalised and forgotten people of society we are welcoming him. And in a sense the Christians in Algeria are on the edge of society – they are marginalised. Lokmane assured Fr Paul that he was welcome as someone who had embraced their culture, and become a bridge builder between two different civilizations, north and south of the Mediterranean:

> You were a stranger and we welcomed you. You were a stranger and our people welcomed you. You were a stranger and Algeria welcomed you. She welcomed you several times. First of all when you did your military service in the aftermath of independence, then when you came to learn her language and

to absorb her culture and finally to live here and teach in one of her universities for thirty years. On no occasion was her door closed to you. Not only did she offer you hospitality but also she adopted you and made you one of her sons, granting you citizenship, fully and entirely. And today you have become, by the grace of God, one of the bishops of her Church.[2]

Lokmane concluded by saying that the Muslim presence at Fr Paul's ordination represented a reaching out in friendship to the people of the north of the Mediterranean from where Fr Paul had come, an act of solidarity 'respecting the beliefs and the convictions' of both cultures 'which are complementary, springs overflowing with life, love and hope'.

To Be the Presence of Christ

The concept of the sacrament of encounter enables Algerian Christians to relate their daily experiences to the Galilean ministry of Jesus, a ministry where for the most part he encountered Jews and Gentiles who didn't become his disciples but who were nevertheless changed by their meeting with him. Father Christoph Theobald, a Jesuit theologian, visited the Algerian Church on seven occasions to help her reflect on her witness in a Muslim context. In his book,[3] *Gospel Presences: Reading the Gospels and the Apocalypse in Algeria and Elsewhere*, he explains that these meetings are healing because through words and gestures the other person is made aware of their own uniqueness. According to Fr Christoph, 'To be the presence of Christ – people in a sacramental relationship – it is finally

---

2. *La Semaine Religieuse d'Alger*, mars (2009), pp. 69–70.

3. Christoph Theobald, *Présences d'Évangile: Lire les Évangiles et l'Apocalypse en Algérie et ailleurs* (Paris: Les Editions de l'Atelier, 2003).

to release that which is more human, it is to allow the person met on the road to have access to their unique humanity, it is at last to discover – in this admirable exchange – one's own humanity.'[4]

The ability to see and understand these daily encounters with people outside the Christian faith as sacramental is vital for those in a totally Muslim society where only very few of those whom they meet will seek admission into the Christian Church. Father Christoph encouraged the Algerian Church by telling her that 'this to-ing and fro-ing between the stories of daily life and the Gospel stories is absolutely essential because it brings forth the spiritual meaning of what you are living; it has the advantage of transforming these situations into the Word or call of God'.[5] And of course this sacramentality of everyday life is a gift of the Spirit which knows no religious or racial boundaries as Jesus showed so clearly in his encounters with Jairus, the Centurion, the woman with the haemorrhage, the Samaritan woman at the well, and many others.

So Very Sorry

Monsignor Alphonse Georger, the Bishop of Oran, in his diocesan magazine, *Le Lien*, recently highlighted a story illustrating Fr Christoph's point.[6] Sister Jeanne had just celebrated her feast day and the following day Mgr Alphonse received a cake from her, which he duly put in the deep freeze to await the next meeting of his Diocesan Council. That same evening he rang Sr Jeanne to thank her for her gift thinking

4. Martin McGee OSB, *Christian Martyrs for a Muslim People* (New York/Mahwah NJ: Paulist Press, 2008), p. 121.

5. Ibid., p. 120.

6. *Le Lien,* février-mars (2008), pp. 3–4. Monsignor Georger retired in 2012 and has been succeeded by Mgr Jean-Paul Vesco OP.

that she had received several cakes for her feast day and had passed on one of them to him. She asked him if he had read the inscription on the cake and he said, 'No'. 'Well read it,' she replied, 'and I'll explain all to you tomorrow.' The bishop, on taking the cake out of its wrapping, discovered these words: 'So Very Sorry.' Monsignor Alphonse eagerly awaited Sr Jeanne's explanation.

From time to time Sr Jeanne goes to a local cake shop to buy some croissants. On each visit the owner has a little chat with her and inquiries about her health and the well-being of the other sisters in the community. Sister Jeanne on this occasion began to tell him about the troubles the Church in Oran had recently been experiencing, including, no doubt, the suspended sentence received by Fr Pierre Wallez. As she spoke, the baker's face clouded over with surprise and sadness but he said nothing. The following day, however, a packet was delivered to her house containing the sponge cake and its expression of sorrow. Bishop Georger comments that such actions touch one's heart and speak louder than the most eloquent discourses on fraternity. Through his actions and words the Muslim baker had very powerfully and simply conveyed God's love to Sr Jeanne and the Christian community in Oran.

An Outpouring of Love

On 24 April 2009 the tiny Christian community in the Diocese of Laghouat-Ghardaïa in Algeria, better known as the Diocese of the Sahara, was greatly distressed by the unexpected death of Br Xavier Habig, a Little Brother of Jesus attached to the Béni Abbès hermitage. Brother Xavier had been run over by a car. The bus being full, he had decided to walk the final fourteen kilometres to Béni Abbès in the dark. No one will ever know why he was walking in the middle of the road at the time of the accident.

Brother Bernard, also a Little Brother of Jesus attached to the same hermitage, recounted in the diocesan magazine[7] the heartwarming response of the local authorities and of the local people. The governor and the deputy governor of the region sent their condolences and the mayor and county manager came in person to offer their sympathy. In addition, the municipality made a house available to accommodate the eleven family members who had travelled from France for the funeral and gave special permission to bury Br Xavier in the courtyard of the hermitage. According to local custom Xavier's body was wrapped in a shroud and buried without a coffin. While all of this was going on their Muslim neighbours provided meals for the crowds of sympathisers.

The day after the burial the family of the driver who had killed Br Xavier met with his relations at the hermitage. His brother, Bruno Habig, was very moved when the family of the driver asked for their forgiveness. Fortunately he had rung his elderly mother in France beforehand and was able to pass on a message from her that she had been thinking a lot about the driver and his family and had prayed for them. 'A rare moment, violent emotion, the certainty that my mother had found the only words to suit the occasion.' Another powerful sacrament of encounter between Muslims and Christians had taken place.

Mutual Openness

In the previous chapter I recounted some examples of the trials and instances of petty harassment that the Algerian Church has been subjected to in recent times. However, these three accounts

---

7. *Lettre du diocese de Laghouat-Ghardaïa*, juin (2009), pp. 4–6.

of Gospel encounters between Algerian Christians and their Muslim neighbours give reasons for hope, hope for the future of the Algerian Church and more generally hope for the future of Christian–Muslim relations. The Church in Algeria has lost all of her wealth and institutional power and so her only wealth now lies in her relationships with the Algerian people. Brother Xavier had drawn near to his Muslim neighbours; he had mastered their language and learned to understand their culture. And they in their turn had loved him. The same challenge of mutual understanding and friendship presents itself to the Church in the West in its relationship with a growing Islamic presence. Monsignor Teissier, who has spent his life among the Muslim people of Algeria, writes: 'Let us think in particular of this beatitude, "I was a stranger and you welcomed me" (Mt 25:35). In the relationship with the other, if it is genuine, there is liberation and an entry into the realm of love that is a gift from God. It is in this mutual openness [between Christian and Muslim] that God brings in his Kingdom.'[8]

---

8. McGee, p. 162.

CHAPTER EIGHT

A Look of Admiration: Friendship, the Core of Inter-religious Dialogue

The close friendship which the monks of Tibhirine had built up over almost sixty years with their Muslim neighbours, had, with the assassination of seven of the community, apparently ended in tragedy and disaster. However, the seeds planted at Tibhirine continue to sprout and bear fruit in unexpected places and in unexpected ways. Their secret – that friendship is the indispensable foundation for fruitful dialogue – continues to inspire many.

The great explorer, hermit and mystic, Blessed Charles de Foucauld (1858–1916), devoted his life to living among the Muslim population of the Sahara Desert in the hope of revealing Christ to them. One of his most oft-quoted phrases is, 'Cry the Gospel with your life.' And this is what Charles tried to do without any seeming success, as during his lifetime he failed to make any lasting conversions. Antoine Chatelard, a Little Brother of Jesus, who has lived at Tamanrasset in the Algerian desert since 1954, has written much about the life and spirituality of Charles. In his book, *Charles de Foucauld: Le chemin vers Tamanrasset*,[1] he traces the evolution of Charles' attitude to the evangelisation of the Muslim nomads, the people among whom he lived 'his hidden life of Nazareth'.

---

1. Antoine Chatelard, *Charles de Foucauld: Le chemin vers Tamanrasset*, (The Road to Tamanrasset) (Paris: Karthala, 2002).

CRY THE GOSPEL WITH YOUR LIFE

On 20 January 1908 Charles notes in his diary that he has fallen seriously ill. He is all alone in his little shack, bedridden and on the point of death. It has not rained for seventeen months and the surrounding countryside is suffering from the effects of famine. The goats are no longer producing any milk, the staple diet of the poor. Brother Charles, having distributed his remaining stock of wheat and dates to the needy, is also short of food. He who had dispensed his riches to the poor of the region has now become one of them, for the first time. The Touaregs, realising Charles' plight, scoured the surrounding countryside in order to find some goat's milk. And having found some of this precious and scarce commodity, they nursed him back to health.

Antoine Chatelard sees this event as a moment of conversion for Charles. Up until then he had thought that he could get along 'without the reciprocity which defines friendship'.[2] Now Charles realises that he needs his Muslim neighbours as much, if not more, than they need him. He begins to make friends with them. 'It had taken this state of exhaustion produced by his illness before his hosts could offer him something and meet him as an equal.'[3] Out of this new relationship Charles saw Muslims differently and could write that he was not there to convert the Touaregs but to understand them as 'I am convinced that God will receive us all [Muslims, Protestants and Catholics] if we merit it.'[4] Friendship by its very nature involves treating others as equals and being prepared both to receive as well as to give.

---

2. Ibid., p. 259.
3. Ibid., p. 258.
4. Ibid., p. 260.

A Spiritual Friendship

Another example of an inspiring inter-religious friendship is also linked to Algeria, this time directly to the monks of Tibhirine. Professor Azzedine Gaci, President of the Regional Council for the Muslim Religion in Lyon, France, was very moved by a film about the life of Br Luc of Tibhirine and his work as a doctor serving the villagers of Tibhirine. Having watched this film Professor Gacci came to see Cardinal Barbarin of Lyon, telling him: 'This man [Br Luc] gave his life to Algeria and offered it in sacrifice. The kidnapping and assassination of the seven monks of Tibhirine is monstrous. Would you agree to go there with me to pray and to ask pardon of God?'[5] Professor Gacci wanted to pray not for the monks who were, he said, undoubtedly in heaven, but rather for the assassins who might be still alive and in need of God's mercy and the grace of conversion. The cardinal immediately replied: 'If you're leaving tomorrow, you can count me in.'

The pilgrimage that the two men, accompanied by seven members of each of their communities, made to Tibhirine in February 2007 was the high point of a friendship and a dialogue that had grown between them over a number of years. As a result of this spiritual friendship they feel free to speak openly to each other about their faith and to share their love of God with each other. The theme of God's mercy, one of the central themes of Islam, has been a key to their spiritual dialogue. Cardinal Barbarin writes: 'One year, at the start of Ramadan, he sent an electronic message to his friends where there was no mention of fasting. This month, he explained, is consecrated to mercy. We pray to ask pardon for our sins and to obtain the purification

---

5. For the full text of Cardinal Barbarin's talk in French, see http://lyon.catholique.fr

of all people. I suggest to those who wish to take part to unite themselves to our spiritual undertaking by the following prayer: "Forgive us our trespasses as we forgive those who trespass against us." When I remarked to him that these are the words of Jesus in the Our Father, he replied: "Yes. I know that very well, but it is the most beautiful prayer for forgiveness that I know of!"'

In the wake of their pilgrimage to Tibhirine, the two communities in the Lyonnais region have come closer together and all the imams and priests of the region have met for a day-long encounter. Subjects such as faith, mercy, almsgiving, pilgrimage, spiritual struggle, and many moral issues have been discussed. The spiritual friendship between the cardinal and Professor Gaci has enabled both men to explore the riches of each other's faith and challenged them to live it with greater fidelity. Cardinal Barbarin writes that in inter-religious dialogue we must move from tolerance to mutual esteem and with God's grace to admiration for one another. 'For the progress of inter-religious dialogue and the spiritual journey of everyone, we need much more [than tolerance]: namely a deep confidence, an interest that comes both from the intelligence and the heart, a look of contemplation and of admiration.' One day Azzedine Gaci asked Philippe Barbarin to explain to him the Christian understanding of the Trinity. The cardinal did his best and was rewarded by an admiring response: 'I knew well that it [your explanation] would be very beautiful.'

I HAVE MORE TO LEARN THAN TO GIVE

Monsignor Claude Rault, a White Father, is Bishop of the Diocese of Laghouat-Ghardaïa in Algeria. His vast diocese of two million square kilometres in the Saharan Desert has only a few hundred Christians, so Bishop Claude has had every opportunity to get to know some of the three and a half million

Muslims who live within his diocesan boundaries! He first arrived in Algeria in September 1970, just eight years after the country had gained its independence from France. His first posting was as deputy director of a centre for professional formation run by the White Fathers. He had no training for this post and felt unsure of himself. To make matters worse, he had also been influenced by the negative image of Algeria and Algerians then prevalent in France. Thus it was that he arrived in Algiers in 1970 with an 'unconscious and insidious fear' of the country, and found himself in charge of a boarding house for sixty Algerians students just a few years younger than himself. Despite gradually becoming more at ease as the months went by, a sense of disquiet persisted and 'hindered that confidence without which no educational project or lasting friendship are possible'.[6]

The breakthrough occurred in a totally unexpected manner. A group of friends came to visit him from France and straight away some of his students invited them to come and see them in their homes. One of the students, Akly, insisted that they come and share a meal of couscous prepared by his mother. His mother had been widowed eight years earlier in 1962 when her husband was killed by the French army, and she now had the generosity of spirit to invite a group of French people into her home. Claude Raoult experienced this act of forgiveness like a:

> liberating electric shock, a kind of healing of memory. Reconciliation is really possible! The proof! It is the start of a relationship that changes the whole meaning of my life. I realise that I have more to learn than to give. The country becomes a part of me. It is as if this woman had brought to birth in me

---

6. Monsignor Claude Raoult, *Désert, ma cathédrale* (Paris: Desclée de Brouwer, 2008), p. 24.

a new life, a new way of seeing, a new relationship. I am freed from all fear. Nothing from now on would be the same. The covenant was made during a shared meal.[7]

Like Charles de Foucauld, Claude has come to realise that his relationship with his Muslim neighbours is one of mutual self-giving and friendship. 'I realise that I have more to learn than to give.' Claude goes on to say that the Christian missionary is not just someone who reveals the love of God to others, in this case Muslims. He is also someone who recognises that God's love precedes his arrival, that God has already been at work among these people. The missionary must recognise that Muslims also 'live an authentic relationship of love with God and with others'.[8] This echoes the Second Vatican Council insight that 'by His incarnation, the Son of God has united Himself in some fashion with every man' (*Gaudium et Spes*, no. 22). Through the incarnation every person, by the very fact of their humanity, enters into a relationship with God through Jesus Christ. The Holy Spirit continues to work through the Church but the Spirit is also active in the hearts of those outside the visible Church who, like this Kabyle woman, 'live an authentic relationship of love with God and with others'.

Christians thinking about reaching out to people of other faiths can take heart from the experience of the Church in Algeria. It teaches us that the first and most important step in dialogue is to stretch out our hands in friendship. As Mgr Claude Raoult puts it: 'Dialogue presupposes the experience of a real encounter, of a gratuitously lived relationship: that of friendship and mutual esteem.'[9]

7. Ibid., p. 25.
8. Ibid., p. 98.
9. Raoult, p. 82.

CHAPTER NINE

Loving Those Who Are Different

Recently I received a letter from a religious sister living in Britain who mentioned that she was becoming afraid of the growing threat of Islam. This sister is a very tolerant and loving person so I imagine that her reaction is not uncommon. We all tend, to some extent at least, to fear what is different and unknown. This is the very reaction we see Jesus dealing with in the Gospels. In the story of the Good Samaritan, Jesus undermines religious and racial prejudice; we can often fail to pick up on the underlying message of many of his encounters on account of our familiarity with them. Jesus has no difficulty in recognising God's presence in the faith of people who are outside the Jewish people, e.g. the faith of the centurion: Matthew 8:10, Luke 7:9 and that of the Syrophoenician woman: Matthew 15:28, Mark 7:29. And, as the parables of the Good Samaritan, Luke 10:25-37, and the Final Judgement, Matthew 25:31-46, make clear, he calls us to love these outsiders.

Monsignor Teissier spells out very clearly the non-sectarian demands of Christian love. He writes:

> The love, which reveals God, is not any old sentiment. It has at least two characteristic features. It is universal and free. To love those of one's own side is in the end to love oneself. But to love without erecting boundaries is to respond to the Sermon on the Mount. 'For if you love those who love you, what reward do you have? Do not even the tax collectors do the same?' (Mt 5:46). The love which reveals the God of the Gospel is one which makes no distinction between people.

It is for this reason that Jesus chose the parable of the Good Samaritan to speak to us about God's way of loving. The Samaritan cares for the wounded Jew. It is moreover what Jesus himself lived out. His love is universal and free. The God of Jesus Christ 'makes his sun to rise on the evil and on the good' (Mt 5:45).[1]

GOD SHOWS NO PARTIALITY

Breaking down the barriers caused by prejudice and fear can happen as a result of a 'Good Samaritan' type of experience transforming our understanding of the other as other. This was the experience of Fr René Robert,[2] a Frenchman and White Father who was sent to work in Algeria in 1965. In 2008, on the sixtieth anniversary of his priestly ordination, he recounted the story of his breakthrough in overcoming his many more or less conscious prejudices against Islam. While working in a White Father school in a suburb of Algiers, René was invited to a meal in the house of one of his teaching colleagues, a very good teacher and devout Muslim. He found himself in the midst of an exemplary family with well brought up children and a united couple. René's moment of breakthrough had arrived:

And I was suddenly flooded by light. How could God not love them? And little by little I understood that what's important before God is not belonging to a certain religion: God loves everyone of good will. What counts is the human value of each person according to the light which they have received. When a person practises submission to God,

---

1. Martin McGee OSB, *Christian Martyrs for a Muslim People* (New York/Mahwah NJ: Paulist Press, 2008), p. 173.
2. Father René died on 8 May 2014 in Algiers at the age of ninety-six.

uprightness, concern for others, how could God not love them? When the mother of a family is completely devoted to her children and full of charity towards others, how could God not love her?[3]

Father René goes on to say that the source of light and truth for him is to be found in Jesus Christ. He is also aware of his responsibility to share these riches with others through the promotion of the values present in St Matthew's parable of the Final Judgement. René's experience could be compared to that of St Peter when he realised that the Gentile centurion, Cornelius, had received the Holy Spirit. He exclaims: 'I truly understood that God shows no partiality, but in every nation anyone who fears him and does what is right is acceptable to God (Acts 10:34).' Father René had come to realise that the Holy Spirit was also active among his Muslim pupils and their families.

Everything Changes in our Relationship

Sister Zawadi, a White Sister from Burkina Faso, also underwent a similar experience of conversion in her relationships with her Muslim neighbours, a conversion in her case from fear to love. The Holy Spirit too had a part to play in her new way of seeing and understanding Islam.

On her arrival in Algeria in 2002, Sr Zawadi's ministry involved working with disabled children and their families, families often given little support by their relatives or society. She experienced quite a culture shock as many Algerians view people from sub-Saharan Africa as second-class citizens and in addition they find it hard to accept that they are not Muslims.

---

3. *La Semaine Religieuse d'Alger* 2 (2008), p. 35.

Feeling inadequate to the challenge of explaining her Christian beliefs to those who confronted her added to the stresses and strains she was experiencing. To make matters worse, the Algerian government, in an effort to appease the Islamists, had introduced new laws in 2006 making Christian worship and practice more difficult. Daunted by living in a society where everything is interpreted within a Muslim framework, her feelings of inadequacy had the unexpected result of forcing her to deepen her own prayer life and spirituality.

An inability on the part of the public authorities to distinguish between the proselytising activity of some evangelicals and the public practice of one's faith was also causing difficulties for the Catholic community. As a result of the change in attitude to the Christian presence by the authorities, Sr Zawadi came under suspicion of using her access to families as a cover for proselytising. She was surprised to discover that she didn't feel any fear upon receiving a summons to go to the police station at El Goléa to explain what she was doing and what she spoke about while visiting the families. Aware of her theological and intellectual limitations, she was obliged to rely more on the Holy Spirit for what she should say and do. She had come to trust in the Spirit's presence in her and in Jesus' words: 'And lo, I am with you always, even unto the end of the world (Mt 28:20).'

The Spirit's presence had also transformed her outlook. She writes: 'To have the Holy Spirit, what does that mean to me? Is it not perhaps to start from the favourable premise that the other does not inevitably wish me ill, that they have a hidden need behind their apparent violence? The Holy Spirit of Jesus inspires us at the right moment, frees us from fear, makes us brothers and sisters.'[4] Through her efforts to overcome her fear of a different culture and religion, Sr Zawadi has discovered common ground and unsuspected values that have drawn her closer to her Muslim neighbours. She concludes: 'The Algerians love us; they only need us to recognise them for who they are, that we respect them. And everything changes in our relationships.'[5]

The Communion of Friendship

Meeting God in Friend and Stranger, a very fine teaching document published by the Catholic Church in England and Wales on inter-religious dialogue, also draws attention to the key role of the Holy Spirit in our relationship with other faiths. It points out that this was a 'remarkable feature' in the teaching of St John Paul II. The bishops state: 'It is the Holy Spirit who is the hidden source of all that is true and holy in them [other religions], and so provides the common ground where each can reach out to the other.'[6] Sister Zawadi makes the same point when she writes: 'In our very differences when we come together in the communion of friendship, the New Creation can come to birth. Something of God is already born. Independently of our human control.'[7]

Fear of Islam is not confined to a few individuals but can be seen on the wider political scene, for example the vote in Switzerland to ban the construction of minarets on mosques. The lively political debate in France, Belgium and elsewhere about wearing the burka also suggests a lurking fear and lack of understanding of the other who is different. To overcome

4. *La Semaine Religieuse d'Alger* 8 (2008), p. 206.
5. Ibid., 207.
6. Catholic Bishops' Conference of England and Wales, *Meeting God in Friend and Stranger* (London: Catholic Truth Society, 2010), no. 98.
7. *La Semaine Religieuse d'Alger* 8 (2008), p. 206.

this fear requires an effort on our part to understand Muslim beliefs. This understanding should be sufficiently empathic for a mainstream Muslim to recognise its expression as reflecting accurately their own beliefs. According to Robert Caspar, 'The major fault lies in subjecting the other to our own categories, deforming their beliefs where necessary or retaining only those elements of their religion which concur with ours. Our aim should be to have a true image of the Muslim, such that he can recognise himself.'[8] It is all too easy for us to caricature the beliefs of those who are different. How would we feel if a Muslim were to take the preaching of the Ulster extremist, Rev. Ian Paisley, during his most belligerent phase, as representative of mainstream Christian teaching?

A Healing Word to Friend and Stranger

Monsignor Claude Rault, Bishop of Laghouat-Ghardaïa in the Algerian Sahara, tells us that our efforts to understand the Muslim other will be regarded with scepticism, even within the Christian community, and we will be accused of naïveté. However, we have no choice in the matter if we wish to remain faithful to the Gospel. The bishop writes: 'It's a matter of the very heart of our Christian vocation; it's a matter also of the condition in which we will leave the earth for future generations. WE HAVE A COMMON FUTURE: it is in keeping with the meaning of peace, of mutual respect, of our belonging to the same one God, of our common concern for the human person: these are the pillars which we can help to build for tomorrow's world.'[9]

---

8. Robert Caspar and Michael Fitzgerald, *Signs of Dialogue: Christian Encounter with Muslims* (Zamboanga City, Philippines: Silsilah Publications, 1992), p. 244.

9. *Billet Mensuel*, Diocèse de Laghouat-Ghardaïa, mars (2010).

On recognising the evident goodness of his Muslim colleague and his family, Fr René came to realise that they were just as much loved by God as he himself was. In the light of this illumination his prejudices crumbled. In her turn Sr Zawadi discovered the presence of the Holy Spirit as the source of the strength that enabled her to overcome her fear and speak a healing word to friend and stranger. She was now free to love those who were different and who at first sight appeared to threaten her own personal identity and faith. They had both discovered in the words of St John Paul II: 'The differences [between human beings] are a less important element, when confronted with the unity which is radical, fundamental and decisive.'[10] And the source of this unity is the Holy Spirit.

---

10. Saint John Paul II's Christmas Address to Roman Curia, no. 3, 22 December 1986, www.ewtn.com

CHAPTER TEN

Surprised by Love: The Heart of Christian-Muslim Dialogue

Together Christians and Muslims make up approximately 55 per cent of the world's population, so good relationships between them are vital for world peace. Given that the media tend to specialise in bad news, most of us only hear about the difficulties in Christian–Muslim relationships and, of course, these difficulties are not hard to find. Even the Arab Spring appears to be mainly bad news for the Christians living in North Africa and the Middle East, especially for the Copts in Egypt.

A low point in Christian–Muslim relationships occurred in September 2006 when Pope Benedict in his Regensburg speech appeared to castigate the Prophet Mohammed. An unfortunate quotation critical of the Prophet led Muslims to think that the pope lacked respect for Mohammed and for their religion. However, good has, in an unexpected manner, come out of that misunderstanding. It has led to two open letters from Muslim scholars, the first addressed solely to Pope Benedict and the second to all Christian leaders. The second letter entitled, *A Common Word Between Us and You*,[1] emphasises the common ground between Islam and Christianity, namely the two great commandments of love of God and love of neighbour.

---

1. The text of this letter can be found in: Miroslav Volf et al., *A Common Word: Muslims and Christians on Loving God and Neighbor* (Grand Rapids/Cambridge: William B. Eerdmans Publishing Company, 2010), pp. 30–50. The book contains many insightful articles by Christian and Muslim scholars in response to the open letter.

In this chapter I examine the content of these two open letters as they show an unexpected breakthrough at the theological level in Christian–Muslim relationships. I will then attempt to put flesh on their outlook by recounting the story of the recently deceased French priest, Fr Pierre Lafitte, who was 'chaplain' to several thousand Muslim students in Algiers and much loved by them. This story will, I hope, provide us with a contemporary example, illustrating the theological insights of *A Common Word Between Us and You*, of how Christians and Muslims can love each other as brothers and sisters.

The Reasonableness of Faith

Pope Benedict in his Regensburg[2] speech was addressing German university intellectuals and appears not to have fully realised the negative impact some of his comments could give rise to when read by a Muslim audience. The focus of his lecture was 'the reasonableness of faith', and he argued that the attempt to separate faith and reason was a great disservice to both. The God of St John's Gospel is the God of logos or reason. What annoyed his Muslim audience was not the pope's linking of faith and reason but rather his reference to the dialogue in 1391 between the Christian emperor Manuel II Palaiologos and an educated Muslim Persian. This dialogue, and the modern Christian commentary on it which the pope quoted, could be seen to imply that Muslims do not see God as bound by reason and that Islam approves of the use of violence to promote conversion. In response to this lecture thirty-eight, leading Muslim intellectuals and religious leaders wrote the first *Open Letter to His Holiness Pope Benedict*[3] on 12

---

2. www.cwnews.com
3. www.monasticdialog.com

October 2006. In it they challenge the accuracy of some of his interpretations of Islam, especially those relating to the use of reason and violence.

For example, they note that 'in their most mature and mainstream forms the intellectual explorations of Muslims through the ages have maintained a consonance between the truths of the Quranic revelation and the demands of human intelligence, without sacrificing one for the other'. They challenge Pope Benedict's quotation that 'for Muslim teaching, God is absolutely transcendent', a statement which they qualify as 'a simplification which can be misleading'. They quote from the Qur'an showing God's closeness to humans, e.g. 'We are closer to him than his jugular vein.' They go on to clarify the meaning of 'jihad' as 'struggle, and specifically struggle in the way of God'. For a war to be considered just, there are stringent conditions that need to be observed. They comment: 'If a religion regulates war and describes circumstances where it is necessary and just, that does not make the religion war-like, any more than regulating sexuality makes a religion prurient.'

The thirty-eight signatories of the open letter endorse Pope Benedict's statement in Cologne on 20 August 2005, that 'Inter-religious and inter-cultural dialogue between Christians and Muslims cannot be reduced to an optional extra. It is, in fact, a vital necessity, on which in large measure our future depends.'[4] They go on to say that for dialogue to be fruitful those engaged in it will need to listen carefully to the way in which believers from the other tradition understand their faith and not rely solely on 'experts' from within their own tradition.

---

4. Ibid.

THE PARAMOUNT IMPORTANCE OF LOVE

Exactly one year after issuing the first letter, a second, longer open letter, *A Common Word Between Us and You*,[5] addressed to the pope and leaders of all the major Christian denominations, was published. The title *A Common Word between Us and You* is taken from the Qur'an 3:64 which encourages Christians and Muslims to at least agree on the necessity of worshipping 'none but God, and that we shall ascribe no partner unto Him'.[6] The one hundred and thirty-eight signatories were representative of Muslim scholars, religious leaders, and intellectuals from forty-three nations and from all the major Islamic traditions. Amazingly, of all the people approached to sign the letter only two declined.[7] The aim of the letter was simply 'to try to spread peace and harmony between Christians and Muslims all over the world'.[8] The intention, says HRH Prince Ghazi of Jordan, was to 'find a theologically correct, pre-existing *essential* common ground (albeit interpreted perhaps differently) between Islam and Christianity, rooted in our sacred texts and in their common Abrahamic origin'.[9] And this common ground, the signatories of the letter believe, is to be found in the unity or oneness of God and in the twofold command of love of God and love of neighbour. The letter is accessible to scholar and non-scholar alike, and the following two quotations give a good flavour of its style and key content.

There are numerous injunctions in Islam about the necessity and paramount importance of love for – and mercy towards

5. Volf, Ibid., pp. 30–50.
6. Ibid., p. 46.
7. Ibid., p. 177.
8. Ibid., p. 9.
9. Ibid., p. 10.

– the neighbour. Love of the neighbour is an essential and integral part of faith in God and love of God because in Islam without love of the neighbour there is no true faith in God and no righteousness. The Prophet Muhammad said: 'None of you has faith until you love for your brother what you love for yourself.' And: 'None of you has faith until you love for your neighbour what you love for yourself'.[10]

Whilst Islam and Christianity are obviously different religions – and whilst there is no minimising some of their formal differences – it is clear that the *Two Greatest Commandments* are an area of common ground and a link between the Qur'an, the Torah and the New Testament. What prefaces the Two Commandments in the Torah and the New Testament, and what they arise out of, is the Unity of God – that there is only one God. ... Thus the Unity of God, love of Him, and love of the neighbour form a common ground upon which Islam and Christianity (and Judaism) are founded.[11]

Some Christian commentators were first of all surprised by the boldness of the Muslim scholars and leaders in associating themselves so closely with the Christian scriptures and its vocabulary, as traditionally Muslims have claimed that the Christian scriptures have been either misinterpreted or corrupted in transmission. Secondly, they questioned whether Christian and Muslims mean the same thing by their use of the word 'God' (whom Christians understand as triune) and of the word 'love'.

---

10. Ibid., pp. 43–4.
11. Ibid., pp. 45–6.

To Come to a Deeper Understanding

In a desire to respond generously to the Muslim initiative, a group of Christian academics published *Loving God and Neighbor Together: A Christian Response to 'A Common Word Between Us and You'* in the *New York Times* on 18 November 2007, just one month after the publication of *A Common Word Between Us and You*. This document is now known as *The Yale Response*.[12] Whilst acknowledging the common ground, *The Yale Response* also recognises the differences and obstacles that lie between the two faiths. They note that to say 'that something is "at the heart" of the Christian faith is not to say that it *is* the heart of the Christian faith. For the Christian, Jesus Christ is the undisputed heart of faith'. The two great commandments do lie, they go on to say, at the heart of Christianity, as does faith 'understood as utter trust in God'.[13]

The Yale Response states that clarification of what Christians and Muslims mean by 'love of God' and 'love of neighbour' and indeed of 'God' and 'neighbour' requires further dialogue. This process is not like a political settlement where both parties give up some of their demands in order to reach a settlement. Truth is at stake and faith convictions cannot be bargained away. 'Instead, in an interfaith encounter we can come to a deeper understanding of our own and the other's convictions and discover that we already agree on more than we originally thought'.[14]

The signatories to *The Yale Response* see the Muslim acceptance of the Christian sacred texts as a big step forward as now 'perhaps Muslims and Christians will be able to return to dialogue focusing on the interpretation of these texts

---

12. See Volf et al., pp. 52–6.
13. Ibid., pp. 57, 58.
14. Ibid., p. 66.

rather than on questions of reliability'.[15] In this respect I was struck by what the Muslim Seyyed Hossein Nasr, Professor of Islamic Studies at George Washington University, had to say in the book *A Common Word* about the teaching of Jesus. He remarks that it is self-evident to Christians that the two great commandments form the basis of Jesus' teaching but what he asks is the Muslim attitude towards them. First he points out that the great commandments are to be found in the Qur'an and Hadīth (i.e. the sayings and life of Muhammad). Furthermore Jesus is regarded by Muslims as a prophet and any teaching by a prophet which has not been 'explicitly abrogated by a later revelation still stands as an expression of truth and God's commandment to and will for Muslims'.[16]

HOPE FOR THE FUTURE

Reading these two open letters gives great hope for the future. After all, those of us brought up as Catholics before the Second Vatican Council will remember how implacably negative at that time were the teachings of the Catholic Church regarding other Christian communities. If I remember correctly, it was a mortal sin to attend a service of another denomination, even a funeral service for a relative. How far we have come in our understanding of and love for other Christians since those unforgiving times. And a similar process appears to be now taking place regarding our understanding of and relationship to other faiths. I think anyone reading the two open letters would be agreeably surprised by how much we hold in common with Muslims. Nevertheless, it will take time for the scholarly breakthroughs to filter down to the man or woman in the local mosque or church.

---

15. Ibid., p. 60.
16. Ibid., p. 115.

The advances in inter-religious understanding shown in the two open letters can be seen to be fleshed out in the life of the recently deceased Fr Pierre Lafitte, particularly in his ministry to Muslim medical students in Algiers. According to Fr Pierre faith 'comes from the heart and if one wishes to understand the believer one must enter into his heart'.[17] And that is why his story is worth hearing because he shows us how the insights of the two open letters can be lived out in daily life.

Serving a Muslim People

Father Pierre was born in 1943 to a devout Catholic family in St Jean de Luz in the French Basque region. In 1963 he went on a summer camp to Algiers to help children with literacy problems and it was there that he fell in love with the Algerian people, a love that was to be richly reciprocated. His early years as a priest were lived out in Algiers among the Muslim poor of the working class district of Belcourt. As well as being a pastor to the tiny Christian community, he devoted himself to literacy work with unemployed adolescents. From 1995 until his death on 30 November 2010 Pierre worked in the Jesuit run CCU (*Centre Culturel Universitaire*) as a librarian serving several thousand Muslim medical students. Through his work he became their de facto chaplain, someone who knew how to love them in good times and bad.

Pierre led a very humble and simple existence and it was only after his unexpected death of a heart attack in November 2010 at the age of sixty-seven that the full impact of his witness became known. The hatred and fanaticism of the Algerian civil war had affected him deeply. Despite the enveloping forces of

---

17. *La Semaine Religieuse d'Alger, Rencontres*, Numéro spécial Pierre Lafitte, Archevêché d'Alger, Janvier (2011), p. 19.

evil, Fr Pierre steadfastly believed that he and others should live fearlessly, taking courage from the lives of those people who, in the words of Camus, 'justify the world' and believing above all that such a person can be found in everyone we meet.[18] His courage and desire to witness to the truth are perhaps best expressed in a reflection he wrote while on pilgrimage to Lourdes in 2003: 'In the evening of my life, in a community ravaged by so much violence ... one conviction: to remain hand in hand with the people of this suffering country, without speaking – Job, silent and faithful.'[19]

The Gift of Self

Of course Fr Pierre did speak! The Algerian Church likes to say that the fifth Gospel everyone can read is the Gospel of our life. And the students whom Fr Pierre served had no difficulty in understanding his witness. This was clearly demonstrated in the outpouring of love that greeted his death. His funeral Mass in the magnificent Cathedral of the Sacré Coeur was full to overflowing with hundreds of his faithful medical students, many of them in tears. The Vicar General, Fr Christian Mauvais, introduced the Muslim participation in the Mass by saying: 'Pierre is a priest, a Christian. His beloved people are Muslim. It is therefore important that the latter express their prayers for Pierre, not apart, outside, but at the heart of our celebration! Let us receive this act of faith from our Muslim brothers and sisters.'[20]

A young lady doctor, Aïcha Naïli, who recited the Muslim prayers for the dead at the mass, said in her tribute:

18. *Rencontres*, p. 15.
19. Ibid., p. 18.
20. Ibid., p. 38.

The first words which resound most strongly in my ears, and above all in my heart, is your oft-used expression 'gift of self'. You remained fascinated by this complete gift of self to the other, which God first gives to us. Therefore as far as you were concerned, we should also act in a similar manner towards our brothers and sisters. If I had to sum up your life, I would say that it was a gift of yourself to the other. This achievement had its foundation in God: If He gives himself to us it's because He loves us. If He gave you this capacity for gift, it's because he had first given you a loving heart. If I am to find the secret of your being, it will be this Loving Heart.[21]

A second equally moving tribute by another young Muslim lady doctor, Lilia, had this to add: 'Every student who knew Pierre remembers him; a warmth which we unwittingly received from him without expecting it … His Love surprised us. When we were sad, struggling, stressed we used to come to the CCU … Pierre's smile, without a word, made all this vanish … hate, sorrow, vileness … all gone. He loved us without reserve and thanks to him we managed to love ourselves "a little".'[22]

Surprised by the Depth of their Love

Do we not find in these eulogies a living example of what love of God and love of neighbour can mean between Muslims and Christians in daily life, a lived expression of the theological understanding that lies behind the two open letters?

I imagine that some of you reading this chapter may be thinking: this is all very fine and good but it has very little to

---

21. Ibid., pp. 29–30.
22. Ibid., p. 35.

do with the lived situation on the ground in so many countries where Muslims treat poorly their Christian minorities and vice versa. This may be true but what the two open letters, and the example of Pierre and his Muslim medical students, hold before us is a picture of how things can change when people open their hearts to each other. And someone has got to take the first step. As Fr Pierre and his Muslim friends have shown us, Christians and Muslims can be surprised by the depth of their love for God and for each other.

CHAPTER ELEVEN

Pierre and Mohamed: No Greater Love

How much Christians and Muslims can love each other was shown poignantly in the lives of Mgr Pierre Claverie, Bishop of Oran, and his young Muslim driver, Mohamed Bouchikhi, both of whom were assassinated on 1 August 1996. The bishop was the last of the nineteen priests and religious to be killed in the Algerian civil war.[1] On that fateful evening Pierre had returned from the capital, Algiers, where he had reluctantly gone to meet the French Foreign Minister, Hervé de Charette, who was on an official visit to war-torn Algeria. On his return to Oran he was met at the airport by Mohamed Bouchikhi, a young Muslim who'd been helping out over the summer at the bishop's house. As they crossed the threshold on reaching home there was a huge explosion. The bishop and Mohamed were killed instantly, their blood mingled in death. Their assassination was not unexpected. Both of them had willingly and knowingly put their lives at risk, Pierre out of love for a Muslim people and Mohamed out of love for his Christian friends. The story of their inspiring witness could hardly be timelier.

---

1. Jean-Jacques Pérennès, has written an excellent biography of Mgr Claverie, *Pierre Claverie: Un Algérien par alliance*, cerf (Paris, 2000). This has been translated into English under the title: *A Life Poured Out: Pierre Claverie of Algeria* (Maryknoll, NY: Orbis, 2007).

Growing Up in a Colonial Bubble

Monsignor Pierre Claverie was born in 1938 in Bab el Oued, a working-class suburb of Algiers, the son of European settlers who had been in Algeria for three generations. He grew up in the 'bulle coloniale', the colonial bubble, with no contact with his Arab neighbours. His family weren't racist but they were indifferent to the surrounding Muslim religion and culture. In a searingly honest letter to his parents in 1960 he wrote, 'We did *nothing*, we the Claverie ... to inform ourselves about the real situation of the Arabs.'[2]

In later life he felt bitter that he could never recall hearing anyone preach in church that the Arabs were also their neighbours and were to be loved too. 'Not to recognise the other side, to pass by without seeing, to live in bubbles, all of that exposes us to explosions of endless violence. I had to cope with the consequences: to try to come out of my bubbles (colonial but also cultural and religious ...), to fight against everything which imprisons and crushes, to open the windows (of the heart and the mind), to pull down the walls which separate ...'.[3]

I Began to Know and Love My Country

After a ten-year sojourn in France training to be a Dominican friar and priest, Pierre returned to an Independent Algeria in 1967 where he found a decimated Catholic community trying very hard to support the fledgling state in its social projects. The Church was seeking to integrate itself into the life of the country, to become *l'Église d'Algérie*, the Church of Algeria, and not the last outpost of a former colonial power. Monsignor

---

2. *Chemins de Dialogue*, numéro 29, Marseille, juin, 2007, p. 167.

3. Ibid., p. 142.

Pierre was up to the challenge and with great enthusiasm he set about learning Arabic, 'the language of the heart', and immersing himself in the literature and traditions of the country. He had the Mediterranean gift for friendship that helped him to enter more fully into the mindset of his fellow Algerians. 'Little by little, a network of human friendships was created and it extended just as much to Christian Arabs as to Muslims; I felt myself "adopted" and I began to know and love my country.'[4]

Pierre quickly succeeded in mastering Arabic and also in coming to grips with the Qur'an. At first the similarities between Christianity and Islam struck him but he quickly came to understand that the same theological words could hide a world of difference. The same words and concepts – revelation, prophet, God's role in creation and history, relationship with God – often had a very different meaning in the other tradition. He came to realise that to make progress in dialogue he had to get to know people in their daily lives, to share common experiences and so have something to build upon. Out of these common commitments, understanding is deepened and a vocabulary can be found 'born of a shared experience'.[5]

I Need the Truth of Others

In the face of these theological differences, Pierre held on to two fundamental intuitions. First, neither side possesses the truth, as the truth is greater than both. So we need to approach the other with an attitude of humility and a willingness to learn. 'I am a believer, I believe that there is a God, but I don't pretend to possess that God, neither through Jesus who reveals him to me,

4. Ibid., p. 143.
5. Ibid., p. 154.

nor through the dogmas of my faith. One doesn't possess God. One doesn't possess truth and I need the truth of others.'[6] It is therefore essential for us to be open to learning from the Muslim other, as well as honestly acknowledging our differences.

Pierre was also committed to a 'plural humanity', that is to say, to the recognition of the diversity and richness of our common humanity. Our differences can become a source of enrichment. 'And this can only come about if each one looks to the other for a portion of the truth and humanity which he lacks. Without this conviction that our humanity is "plural" and enriches itself from the others' difference, without the will to welcome these differences, we fall back on the closed space which we baptise as "authenticity", with its sociological corollary of nationalism.'[7] And among the riches that we can receive from Islam, he notes, is their strong sense of community and solidarity as well as the importance they give to daily prayer in their personal and communal lives.

On the outbreak of the civil war in 1992, Pierre, as Bishop of Oran, fearlessly denounced violence thereby putting his life at risk. When the first two religious, Sr Paul-Hélène and Br Henri Vergès, were assassinated in the Kasbah of Algiers on 8 May 1994, Pierre was scathing in his denunciation: 'What abominable cowardice on the part of these killers of the shade! ... That I should be taken as a target I can understand ... I have always worked tirelessly for dialogue and friendship between peoples, cultures and religions. All of that probably merits death and I am ready to assume the risk. ... But to attack Br Henri and Sr Paul-Hélène, I can't understand it.'[8]

---

6. Ibid., p. 173.
7. Ibid., p. 154.
8. Ibid., p. 174.

PUTTING HIS LIFE ON THE LINE

The life and witness of Pierre and the other eighteen Algerian martyrs live on in surprising ways. No one could have predicted that a play written by Br Adrien Candiard OP, *Pierre & Mohamed,* about the friendship between Pierre and his young Muslim driver Mohamed Bouchikhi would prove to be a runaway success. It was first staged, to critical acclaim, at the Avignon Festival in 2011. Since then it has toured the length and breadth of France and elsewhere to full houses. *Pierre & Mohamed* is a monologue *à deux* where each character in turn reflects upon what it means to engage in dialogue and share friendship with the other.

Who was Mohamed? And why was he willing to run the risk of being assassinated by Muslim extremists on account of his friendship with Pierre? Mohamed was the second of eight children and the oldest male member of his family. A native of Sidi-Bel-Abbès, his family lived next door to the presbytery and the convent. Mohamed became great friends with the parish priest, Fr René You, and with the sisters. Mohamed liked to help out in any way he could, always asking the same question: 'Have you need of anything?' His personality, according to Fr René, could be seen above all in his eyes 'which radiated permanently a smile, gentleness, the greatness of his soul or the breadth of his heart'. When his father threw the whole family out of their home, Fr René gave them refuge in the presbytery for a year. This generosity, no doubt, further strengthened Mohamed's friendship with the Christian community.[9]

In the summer of 1996, Pierre's driver was on holiday and Mohamed willingly responded to Mgr Claverie's request that he should take his place. He knew, of course, that he was putting

---

9. *La vie spirituelle*, no. 721, Septembre, 1997, p. 572.

his life on the line. Just a few months earlier the seven monks of Tibhirine had been kidnapped and beheaded. On agreeing to become his driver he had said, 'I'm doing it because I love you, but I'm going to be killed.'[10] Unfortunately, Mohamed's premonition was to be fulfilled.

Peace Be With You

Brother Adrien in writing the play drew on the homilies and writings of Mgr Claverie and on the short account of Mohamed's life provided by Fr René. Adrien portrays Mohamed as someone who recognises Mgr Pierre's love for him and for the Algerian people. This gratuitous love for himself and the Algerian people astounds and puzzles him. In this short play Br Adrien succeeds marvellously in portraying the spontaneity of Mohamed and his innocent goodness. However, the key to understanding Mohamed's personality and motivation is given to us in a short document that he wrote a few days before his assassination, his final testament. This document allows us to discover the richness of his inner life and shows clearly that he was offering his life freely out of love for his Christian friends. The key words are peace, thanks and forgiveness; and the text is suffused with a feeling of gratitude for all that life had given him. His God is both a God of 'omnipotence' and of 'tenderness'.

In the Name of God, the Clement, the Merciful One.
Before taking up my pen, I say to you: Peace be with you. I thank you who will read my diary and I offer my thanks to everyone who has known me in my life. I say that God will reward them on the last day. Farewell to anyone to whom I may have done harm, may they forgive me. May whoever forgives

10. Ibid., p. 667.

me be forgiven on the day of judgement; and whomever I
may have harmed may he forgive me. I ask forgiveness from
anyone who has heard me say a wicked word, and I ask all
my friends to forgive me on account of my youth. However,
on this day on which I am writing to you, I remember all
the good things that I have done in my life. May God, in
his omnipotence, grant me the gift of obedience to Him and
may He bestow on me his tenderness.[11]

The Real Encounter Which Dialogue Demands

It wasn't easy for Pierre Claverie, a fourth generation European
native of Algeria, to let go of the entrenched attitudes of
the colonisers, of the blindness which failed to register the
existence of the Arab other. Living in the colonial 'bubble'
one didn't meet the other 'except as part of the landscape or
the scenery' (*Pierre & Mohamed*). However, the real encounter
that dialogue demands can only happen if friendship exists
between the partners. 'Dialogue cannot begin yet, he told me,
because before dialogue can take place, friendship has to be
established. A friendship which allows a truthful word, a word
which listens, a word which doesn't deny the other by trying
to convince him, that's what he [Pierre Claverie] had come to
live out in Algeria' (*Pierre & Mohamed*). And the challenge for
Pierre and Mohamed, which Br Adrien presents in the play, is
to acknowledge each other's existence and to love each other,
different but equal. This does not require either of them to
repudiate their own identity but to be open to being enriched
by their differences and to cultivate what they have in common.

Pierre exclaims: 'If I only see you as a Muslim, and if you
only see me as a Christian, then I can no longer encounter

---

11. *La vie spirituelle*, no. 721, Septembre, 1997, p. 573.

Mohamed and you will never know Pierre. And I will never succeed in understanding who you are, nor how you pray to God' (*Pierre & Mohamed*). In other words, the foundation of all dialogue and of all human relationships is the recognition of the humanity of the other. The 'plural humanity', of which Mgr Pierre speaks, recognises the unity and the complementarities of the human race, despite differences of colour, religion or culture.

How did Mohamed, a young man of twenty-one, manage to overcome all those barriers of religion, culture and race in his friendship with Pierre and the Christian community, surrounded as he was by violence, hatred and extremism on all sides? Where did he find the confidence and the love to forge a relationship stronger than death? In his friendship with Fr René and the sisters of Sidi-Bel-Abbès, and later with Pierre, Mohamed must have glimpsed the 'tenderness' of God to which he refers in his testament. And he responded faithfully to this experience with the gift of his life.

INNOCENT VICTIMS OF FANATICISM

Brother Adrien quotes an extract from a homily given by Mgr Claverie in Oran Cathedral on 9 October 1981. This reflection, given a decade before the Islamist armed struggle began in Algeria, is relevant more than ever today as Western society strives to find a way of responding to the fanatical wing of Islam, especially in the aftermath of the *Charlie Hebdo* massacre in Paris. It sums up beautifully one of the key messages of *Pierre & Mohamed*.

I fear nothing more than sectarianism and fanaticism, especially religious. Our Christian history carries many traces of this and it's not without anxiety that we see the development of fundamentalist movements. They are already dividing the Church. In Islam, under the name of the Muslim Brotherhood, they appear to be extending their influence. I know enough Muslim friends, who are also my brothers, to think that Islam knows how to be tolerant, fraternal and concerned to humanise the world by giving it a soul and a heart. They also suffer from seeing the spirit of the mission of their Prophet disfigured by the blind violence of ignorant people and political manipulation. Brothers and friends, let us know how to suffer with them. Let us not reject Islam on account of fanatics who serve it badly. Millions of Algerians live humbly out of this faith, find in it the courage to live an existence which is often difficult, in hope of God's judgement and of better days, and the strength to fight daily against all kinds of enslavement.

Let us have confidence in those thousands of anonymous people who suffer more than we do from all these excesses. As for me, and notwithstanding the fear of difficult times ahead, I am convinced that fanaticism condemns itself by its very excesses.[12]

Innocent victims of fanaticism, Pierre and Mohamed continue to inspire many who work for understanding and friendship between Christians and Muslims. The 'greater love',[13] shown by the laying down of their lives for their friends, is still bearing fruit, not least among those who have watched the play *Pierre & Mohamed*.

---

12. The whole of this homily can be found in French in *La vie spirituelle*, no. 721, septembre, 1997, pp. 775–8.
13. See John 15:13.

CHAPTER TWELVE

Love Hopes All Things: What Future for Christian–Muslim Relations?

Since the start of 2015 it has been quite difficult to open an English language newspaper without finding a story about Muslim extremism and violence. All of these stories help to create a sense of pessimism regarding the future of Christian–Muslim relations. While the omnipresence of the media in today's world has enabled Christians and Muslims to get to know each other better, this is a mixed blessing.

The most recent Church document on inter-religious dialogue, *Dialogue in Charity and Truth*,[1] declares that while on the one hand the development of the means of communication allows various cultures and faith communities to get to know and appreciate each other better, it can also have the unfortunate effect of focusing attention on, and exaggerating, inter-communal and religious problems: 'While this phenomenon of coming together [thanks to the media and ease of travel] can be considered a positive one, it also creates opportunity for the globalisation of once localised problems such as misunderstanding and intolerance in society...'.[2]

The unfortunate truth is that we human beings appear to be attracted more by bad news than good. Thus all the good news about Muslims reaching out to Christians and vice versa will not, as a rule, make the headlines. To give a concrete example,

---

1. *Dialogue in Charity and Truth* published by the Pontifical Council for Interreligious Dialogue on 19 May 2014: www.dimmid.org
2. Ibid., paragraph 4.

Mgr Teissier in a conference in 2008 at Heythrop College, University of London, told a moving story of how a Muslim stood up to Islamic intolerance and risked his life on behalf of his Christian neighbours.

> Quite recently, a religious sister went to buy something from a Muslim shop [in Algiers] near the place where she works and which is the very place where a religious brother and sister, Fr Henri Vergès and Sr Paul-Hélène, were assassinated on 8 May 1994. The shopkeeper told her that he had known them both very well and that he had spoken on television, after their assassination, about the human and spiritual values which they had shown in their lives. Three days later, an assassin came to the shop and killed his brother who happened to be serving behind the counter. This was to punish the family for having given this testimony. This incident shows that Muslims, too, can even risk their lives to pay homage to a Christian.[3]

This is just one story among many which will not make the headlines.

Recognising Each Other Simply as Believers

However, Christian hope is based on something deeper than the latest newspaper reports on Christian–Muslim relations. It is a hope founded on the life, death and resurrection of Jesus of Nazareth whose sacrificial death on the cross empowers us to reach out in love to others. It was his life of sacrificial love for all which inspired the monks of Tibhirine to freely offer their lives

---

3. Henri Teissier, *The Christian Church and Islam: An Algerian Point of View*, Heythrop College, 30 October 2008.

for the sake of their Muslim friends. And we need to recall, in the midst of this media whirlwind of bad news, that the vast majority of Muslims wish to live at peace with their neighbours, whatever their religious label may be. As Mgr Landel, the Archbishop of Rabat in Morocco, reminds us: 'Our Muslim brothers and sisters are also people of prayer; they are also searching for God.'[4]

Faced with a growing indifference to religious belief and an attempt to sideline it from the public square in the developed world, I would argue that our natural allies are to be found among the moderate majority of practising Muslims. As Mohammed Talbi, a Tunisian Muslim, puts it so well, it is no longer 'different concepts of God and the way in which to serve him' which divides followers of different faiths. The division lies rather between those who 'are striving to attain man's destiny without God, and those who can conceive of man's future in and through God'.[5] The recent open letter of the one hundred and thirty-eight Muslim Scholars to Pope Benedict and other religious leaders, *A Common Word Between Us and You,*[6] is evidence of a growing understanding, at least among the religiously educated, of the values we hold in common and of how they can be shared to build a stronger civil society. Of course, all of these hopes for better understanding and mutual appreciation are being endangered by the running sore of the Israeli–Palestinian conflict; a conflict that continues to fuel the rise of radical Islamism.

Monsignor Michael Fitzgerald and Fr Robert Caspar have commented that it has taken five to six centuries for Catholics to see Orthodox and Protestant firstly as fellow

---

4. http://catholique-valence.cef.fr
5. Jo O'Donovan, *Understanding Differently Christianity and the World Religions* (Dublin: Veritas Publications, 2012), p. 172.
6. *A Common Word Between Us and You,* The Royal AAL-BAYT Institute for Islamic Thought, Jordan, 2009 www.acommonword.com

Christians, brothers and sisters in Christ, and secondly as 'non-Catholics'. They continue: 'Is it not time now, when the number of true believers would seem to be decreasing, and when we are faced with the same problems of unbelief and materialism, that Christians and Muslims should consider each other, meet together and collaborate simply as believers, before paying attention to the fact that they are Christians and Muslims?'[7]

The Presence of the Holy Spirit in Every Person

The new theological understanding of the Second Vatican Council has enabled Catholics to dismantle centuries-old barriers of fear and suspicion vis-à-vis Islam. The acceptance by the Church of the activity of the Holy Spirit outside the visible boundaries of the Church, and the recognition of the genuine search for God by Muslims have opened wide the doors to a better understanding and acceptance of the gifts which Islam has to offer. In paragraph nineteen of the latest Vatican Document on inter-religious dialogue, *Dialogue in Charity and Truth*, we read: 'It is the Holy Spirit himself, at work in the heart of every person, who guides the Church to recognise his presence and action in the world even beyond her visible boundaries. Although the Spirit "manifests himself in a special way in the Church and in her members", his presence and activity are universal, limited by neither space nor time and they affect not only individuals but also societies, peoples, cultures and religions as well as history itself.'[8]

However, undoubtedly, the boldest and most fruitful statement of Church teaching is to be found in the Council

---

7. *Signs of Dialogue: Christian Encounter with Muslims* (Zamboanga City, Philippines: Silsilah Publications, 1992), p. 245.
8. *Dialogue in Charity and Truth,* no. 19.

Document *Gaudium et Spes*, no. 22. This teaches that all the benefits of the paschal mystery, which restores humankind to the likeness of God and bestows the new life of the resurrection, are also open to all people of goodwill: 'All this holds true not only for Christians but also for all people of good will in whose hearts grace is active invisibly. For since Christ died for everyone, and since all are in fact called to one and the same destiny, which is divine, we must hold that the Holy Spirit offers to all the possibility of being made partners, in a way known to God, in the paschal mystery.'[9]

This clear teaching of *Gaudium et Spes* about the presence of the Holy Spirit in all people of goodwill contains the theological key to promoting closer relationships between Christians and Muslims. The Holy Spirit, the Spirit of unity, operative in the world both inside and outside the visible boundaries of the Church, reconciles people and faiths to each other. It is the Spirit who enabled the monks of Tibhirine to reach out to their Muslim neighbours, and empowered their neighbours to respond in like manner. It is this same Holy Spirit who enables the members of the *Ribât* to continue to this day to share their common search for God. And precisely because Christians and Muslims are both bearers of God's Holy Spirit they have drawn closer to each other in the sacrament of encounter, in the mutual gift of self. The key challenge which the example of the North African Church poses to Christians and Muslims worldwide is: will you begin to discover God's presence in each other, to love each other as children of the same Father, or will you retreat into your ghettoes of suspicion and recrimination?

---

9. Austin Flannery OP, general editor, *The Basic Sixteen Documents, Vatican Council II*, *Gaudium et Spes*, 22 (Dublin: Dominican Publications, 1996), p. 186.

HOPE FOR THE FUTURE: THE DIALOGUE OF SPIRITUAL
EXPERIENCE

The progress of Christian–Muslim dialogue is difficult to
predict, as the Holy Spirit is not a prisoner of our thinking and
institutions. As Jesus tells a puzzled Nicodemus in St John's
Gospel: 'The wind blows where it chooses, and you hear the
sound of it, but you do not know where it comes from or where
it goes. So it is with everyone who is born of the Spirit' (3:7-8).
The progress of dialogue will, I think, depend to a large extent
on Christians and Muslims, in obedience to the promptings of
the Spirit, learning above all to share their search for God.

The dialogue of spiritual experience allows the participants
to avoid becoming bogged down by contentious theological
issues. Coming together to share the fruits of a common search
for God and 'praying together' allow believers, following the
example of the members of the *Ribât*, to avoid focusing on what
divides them doctrinally. Instead, a sharing of their spiritual
journeys allows participants to experience a sense of fellowship
and unity through the presence of the Holy Spirit. As St John
Paul II stated: 'We can indeed maintain that every authentic
prayer is called forth by the Holy Spirit, who is mysteriously
present in the heart of every person.'[10]

There has been much discussion of the validity of praying
together since St John Paul II organised the first World Day of
Prayer for Peace in Assisi on 27 October 1986 which was attended
by more than one hundred religious leaders of Christian
communities and various world religions. The distinction is
made between 'coming together to pray' and 'praying together'.
In other words, we can prayerfully be present at prayer meetings

10. Saint John Paul II's Christmas Address to Roman Curia, 22 December
1986: www.ewtn.com.

where we each take it in turn to pray whereas joining in each other's prayer, 'praying together' is more problematic.

Pope Benedict XVI lays down three conditions for praying together, rather than just assisting at each other's prayer, if we are to avoid relativism. Firstly, we need to agree on 'who or what God is' and agree that we are talking to a God 'who is able to hear and take notice'. Secondly, we need to agree on 'what is worth praying about and what might be the content of prayer'. And finally: 'The thing must be so arranged that the relativistic misinterpretation of faith and prayer can find no foothold in it.'[11] However, the recent Vatican document *Dialogue in Truth and Charity: Pastoral Orientations for Interreligious Dialogue* strongly discourages people of different religions 'praying together' as they 'differ in their understanding of God'. The document concedes the possibility that believers might 'on very exceptional occasions … be in each other's presence while praying, without actually praying in common' (cf. paras. 82–3). The example of the *Ribât* and the experience of the monks of Tibhirine would, however, indicate that the sharing by Christians and Muslims of their spiritual search for God is a powerful way of coming to recognise God's presence in each other, what St John Paul II calls: 'This radiant mystery of the created unity of the human race, and of the unity of the salvific work of Christ.'[12]

HUNGRY FOR THE SPIRIT

In his first encyclical letter *Redemptor Hominis*,[13] St John Paul II wrote that we are living in 'a time particularly hungry for the

11. Joseph Cardinal Ratzinger, *Truth and Tolerance: Christian Belief and World Religions* (San Francisco: Ignatius Press, 2004), pp. 108–9.

12. Pope John Paul II's Christmas Address to Roman Curia, no. 4.

13. *Encyclical Redemptor Hominis* (London: Catholic Truth Society, 1979).

Spirit, because it is hungry for justice, peace, love, goodness, fortitude, responsibility, and human dignity' (no. 18). This hunger for the Spirit, and the recognition by the Second Vatican Council of his presence in other religions, is the ultimate reason why I am optimistic about progress in Christian–Muslim relations. The Holy Spirit who is secretly at work in the hearts of all people of goodwill will continue to produce a harvest.

Hope for the future is also built on the little actions of everyday life that are open to everyone. As the Vatican document *Dialogue and Proclamation* made clear in its outline of the four pathways of dialogue, everyone can follow at least one of these, the dialogue of daily life, of being a good neighbour. And perhaps this is the simplest and most important message the monks of Tibhirine and the North African Church have taught us by their courageous and persevering commitment to the 'sacrament of encounter'.

Christian–Muslim relationships will improve when we take the trouble to get to know one another as neighbours. They will thrive when we begin to see the Holy Spirit fashioning the image and likeness of God in each other. And at the heart of sincere dialogue between believers in the one God there lies love, because as the First Letter of St John teaches us: 'Everyone who loves is born of God and knows God' (4:7).

APPENDICES

Testament of Christian de Chergé

When an À-Dieu is envisaged …

If it should happen one day – and it could be today – that I should be a victim of the terrorism that now seems to want to embrace all foreigners living in Algeria, I would like my community, my Church, my family to remember that my life was GIVEN to God and to this country.

May they accept that the sole Master of all life was no stranger to this brutal departure. May they pray for me: how could I be found worthy of such an offering? May they know how to associate this death with so many others just as violent, left to the indifference of anonymity.

My life has no more value than any other. It has no less value either. In any case, it has not got the innocence of childhood. I have lived long enough to know that I am an accomplice of the evil that seems, alas, to prevail in the world, and even of that which would blindly strike me.

I would like, when the time comes, to have a moment of lucidity which will allow me to ask pardon of God and of my fellow human beings, while at the same time to pardon with all my heart the person who would strike me down.

I could never wish for such a death; it is important for me to state this. I don't see how I could in fact rejoice that this people whom I love should be accused indiscriminately of my murder.

It is too high a price to pay for what will perhaps be called the 'grace of martyrdom', to owe it to an Algerian, whoever he may be, especially if he claims to be acting out of fidelity to what he believes to be Islam.

I know the contempt with which Algerians in general have been treated. I know also the caricatures of Islam that a certain type of Islamism encourages. It is too easy to salve one's conscience by identifying this religious way with the fundamentalist beliefs of its extremists.

Algeria and Islam are for me something else; they are a body and soul. I have proclaimed this enough, I think, considering what I have received from them, finding there so often that straight guideline of the Gospel learned at my mother's knees, my very first Church, as it so happens in Algeria, and already at that time respectful of Muslim believers.

My death will of course prove right those who have dismissed me as naïve or idealistic: 'Let him tell us now what he thinks about it!' But those people must know that at last my most burning curiosity will be satisfied. I'll now be able, should it please God, to immerse my gaze in that of the Father in order to contemplate with him his children of Islam as he sees them, completely illuminated by Christ's glory, fruit of his Passion, filled by the gift of the Spirit whose secret joy it will always be to establish communion and to re-establish likeness, while playing with the differences.

For this life lost, totally mine and totally theirs, I give thanks to God who seems to have willed it entirely for that special JOY, against and in spite of all odds.

In this THANK YOU in which all of my life is now said, I include of course you, friends of yesterday and today, and you, O my friends of this place, alongside my mother and my father, my sisters and my brothers and their families, the hundredfold granted as it was promised.

And you also, friend of the last moment, who will not have known what you were doing. Yes, for you also I want to say THANK YOU and this À-DIEU to you in whom God's face can be contemplated. And may we be lucky enough to meet again, happy good thieves, in paradise, should it please God, the Father of both of us. Amen! Inch'Allah!

If the Other Were Really to Become My Brother

A reflection[1] by Mgr Vincent Landel, Archbishop of Rabat, Morocco, on the controversy surrounding the caricatures of the Prophet Mohammed in February 2006.

And if the other were really to become my brother! That's the question which we need to ask ourselves at this time when we are invited to recognise a common vocation. Isn't this the question to ask oneself faced with this debate which is all over the media? If the other were really to become my brother, could I call in question the faith that gives him life? Could I trample upon, in one way or another, his beliefs? If the other were really to become my brother, could I speak of freedom without showing respect? If the other were really to become my brother, could I reject him by acting violently against his person or his property? If the other were really to become my brother, could I allow myself to speak negatively about him behind his back? Could I allow myself to annihilate him even in his inner self?

If the other were really to become my brother, I could meet him in truth; we could speak plainly even if we don't always agree. If the other were really to become my brother, meeting him would make me grow; and I am sure that he would grow too. If the other were really to become my brother, our eyes could meet, and a real smile would light up our faces. If the other were really to become my brother, what an exciting world we could build!

---

1. www.valence.cef.fr

These words, written during the period of tension surrounding the 'caricatures', can they not express this common vocation which we share, Muslims and Christians, to be brothers and to become more and more brothers? Have we not got a vocation to be 1) believing brothers; 2) praying brothers; 3) committed brothers?

To Be Believing Brothers

That's what St John Paul II invited us to be when he addressed in 1985 the young Muslims gathered in the Casablanca stadium.

> First of all, I invoke the Most High, the all-powerful God who is our creator. ... He asks every man to respect every human creature and to love him as a friend, a companion, a brother. He invites us to help him when he is wounded, when he is abandoned, when he is hungry and thirsty, in short, when he no longer knows where to find his direction on the pathways of life. Yes, God asks that we should listen to his voice. He expects from us obedience to his holy will in a free consent of mind and of heart. God ... pardons and shows mercy. ... For his blessing and for his mercy, we thank him, at all times and in all places.[2]
>
> We, believers, know that we do not live in a closed world. We believe in God. We are worshippers of God. We are seekers of God.[3]

Our common vocation: isn't it to be worshippers of God, seekers of God? And that is lived out in the everyday. To be believing brothers who do not seek to find lots of differences

2. www.vatican.va
3. Ibid., no. 10.

which could set us apart, but who quite simply, with what we are, put ourselves in a position to grow before God, put ourselves in a position to be true seekers of God. I like very much the relationship between Fr Christian and Mohammed. Mohammed had asked Fr Christian to teach him how to pray; as they often met, a spiritual friendship developed. They had agreed that their encounters would allow them 'to dig this well of knowledge'. And one day as a joke Christian said to Mohammed: 'At the bottom of our well what will we find? Muslim water or Christian water?' and Mohammed replied: 'You know at the bottom of this well what one finds is God's water.' Isn't it this water of God that quenches our thirst? We search for it each in our own way; but we search for it and we help each other to search for it.

About this relationship with God, Christians and Muslims, do we not have to keep on reminding ourselves that the world is a gift God has given to humanity? Thus we are invited to look upon each aspect of this world as something worthy of being discovered and admired. Are we not invited to be together admirers of all that is created? Are we not invited together to praise God for all that is created? Are we not invited to have an a priori confidence in the world and in life?

Our common vocation as believing brothers: is it not to really welcome the world as this gift that God continues to give us every day? To welcome, and at the same time to help others to welcome the reality of this world, not seeing it as an obstacle on our path as people and believers, but as a privileged way to deepen our knowledge of God, our relationship with God. Our common vocation as believers: is it not to believe that this world has been entrusted to the responsibility of humankind? Humans enjoy the very real possibility of managing it for better or for worse. It is a common vocation; it is at the same time a common responsibility.

Our common vocation as believers invites us to accept humans as being creatures of God, whatever their qualities or failings, their race or religion, their social condition or age; creatures whose dignity comes from God. Thus every human being has a sacred value, and this justifies equality between people as they have the same fundamental rights, such as liberty and justice. To follow this path is a common vocation and at the same time a common responsibility. As St John Paul II affirms: 'we, believers, know that we do not live in a closed world. We believe in God. We are worshippers of God. We are seekers of God.'[4] Our vocation to be believing brothers, isn't it an invitation to have a lucid and optimistic view of the world and of the human person? When this happens we will be able to live out our relationships in truth.

To Be Praying Brothers

When the bell of the monastery is joined to the call of the muezzin are we not invited to think that each of us, Muslim and Christian, are summoned to an encounter with God? We are invited to leave behind our activity in order to prepare ourselves to listen, to adore, to be receptive. It's true that we each do it in our own way, but can our hearts not be at one? It is only God who can call to prayer. 'We can say that if this sign of prayer were missing, our Church would be mutilated and also Christian–Muslim dialogue in its present approach would be laborious and difficult' (Fr Christian).

Isn't it Fr Christian who often recalled that the monks of Tibhirine had the vocation of being men of prayer in the midst

---

4. Ibid., no. 4.

of a people of prayer, prayer which joins us at the same time to God and to our Muslim brothers? And Fr Christian stated, 'when one begins to listen honestly to another people at prayer one discovers that the most basic attitudes and words of the spiritual life are unconcerned about religious frontiers. This will show itself by a deep bond in prayer with other people and other believers. I know a communion there which goes beyond frontiers'.

Our Br Jean-Pierre (the older who is at Midelt) has this to say:

> In Morocco we drink tea every day with our neighbours, an encounter of the heart, whose impact, humanly speaking, one can't fully measure. The secret of this encounter lies in prayer. At Tibhirine, the bells of the monastery rang out and the Muslims never asked us to silence them. We respected each other at the very heart of our common vocation: to adore God, to praise him, to sing his glory … Fidelity to the time of prayer is the secret of our friendship with Muslims. With them we wish to put ourselves in God's presence, to be true to ourselves in this interior light which silence permits … our Christian distinctiveness is to believe that God gives us his spirit and makes us live with his life: therein lies our witness.[5]

Isn't the experience of the *Ribât* a response to this vocation of being people of prayer! At the beginning, this encounter was confined to Christians who sought a better understanding of how their prayer could be rooted in the context of their lives in Algeria. Then gradually Muslims were invited to these times

---

5. *La Vie*, no. 3165, 27 avril 2006.

of sharing, prayer and silence, in a spirit of spiritual solidarity. And then, from guests, the Muslims became partners in a more genuine sharing without papering over the differences. In living this out, in the footsteps of the participants of the *Ribât*, can we not say that 'our differences can be regarded as a communion'?

Our common vocation to be praying brothers, does it not respond to the invitation given by St John Paul II to the young people at Casablanca: 'Dear young people, I wish that you may be able to help in thus building a world where God may have first place in order to aid and to save mankind.'?[6]

To Be Committed Brothers
In an unvarying message St John Paul II reminds the young Muslims, but also all people of goodwill:

> God does not will that people should remain passive. He entrusted the earth to them that together they should subdue it, cultivate it, and cause it to bear fruit. ... It is by fully and courageously undertaking your responsibilities that you will be able to overcome the existing difficulties. It reverts to you to take the initiatives and not to wait for everything to come from the older people and from those in office. You must build the world and not just dream about it.[7] God has given the earth to mankind as a whole in order that people might jointly draw their subsistence from it.[8]

This message is also addressed to young Christians. Christians and Muslims, have we not received this common vocation to be

---

6. Saint John Paul II, Casablanca, no. 10.
7. Ibid., no. 7.
8. Ibid., no. 8.

'committed' brothers; not because we wish to gain some profit or other from this world, but because we agree to believe that it has been entrusted to us to be made fruitful; we agree to believe that it has been entrusted to us by God so that it might be 'worthy of Him'; we agree to welcome it in its concrete reality with its riches and its shadows? Believers, we become together responsible for its evolution, its construction, its beauty; believers, we agree to commit ourselves to social, political, economic responsibilities so that every person will be respected in their dignity, in their liberty.

> With all people of goodwill, Christians have to commit themselves to all the tasks that enable people to grow and the world to develop. For development occurs: wherever people are committed to their true vocation; wherever they are loved; wherever they create communities in which they learn to love their family, voluntary groups, nations. People grow and the world develops: wherever the poor person is treated as a human being; wherever adversaries are reconciled; wherever justice is promoted, where peace is established, where truth, beauty and goodness enable people to grow. Christians fulfil their mission as human beings and as Christians, every time that they become involved with other people of goodwill.[9]

Faced with such a programme of love, justice, forgiveness, respect – who could say that it doesn't involve everyone? Can there be specialists in such and such a field; in the technical

---

9. 'Chrétiens au Maghreb – Le Sens de nos Rencontres' (Christians in the Maghreb – The Meaning of our Encounters) *Documentation Catholique*, 1775 (1979), pp. 1032–44.

sphere undoubtedly, but in those fields which require a human and spiritual maturity, surely not? Is not every person of goodwill entrusted with such a responsibility? Every person who wishes to live out his relationship with the world while at the same time respecting his relationship with God, while wishing to live out intensely his faith, is aware of a kind of vocation to act, by looking at reality in a different way, by having a different approach. God cannot become central in one's life without one's participation. A person cannot be seen as a creature of God without a profound experience of God. Isn't it then that we feel that we have received a common vocation, Christians and Muslims, to be 'committed' brothers in this world where, for numerous reasons, we are immersed? Our faith in God gives us a new way of looking at things. To be believers and people of prayer doesn't take on its full meaning until in our own situation we respond to our common vocation to be 'committed' brothers. By respectfully welcoming each other in our common vocation, we will help each other to be faithful to our common vocation; it is then that the other can become my Brother.

Thanks,

Aiguebelle, 28 May 2006
Mgr Vincent Landel SCJ

APPENDIX THREE

A Doctrinal Note on How Christians and Muslims Speak of God: The French Bishops' Conference[1]

Straight away one thing must be recognised: Christians and Muslims (and Judaism must also be included) are monotheistic religions. The Christian creed starts with these words: 'I believe in one God' and the Muslims declare: 'No other god except God' (Allah). The Declaration of the Second Vatican Council on non-Christian religions declares: 'The church has also a high regard for the Muslims. They worship God, who is one, living and subsistent, merciful and almighty, the Creator of heaven and earth, who has also spoken to humanity.'[2]

1. It is right straight away to make clear from which point of view we are speaking about God. If it is a question of the God with whom the human creature is in a relationship through the act of faith, prayer, the desire to accomplish his will, to please him and even to love him (which is true of the mystical current in Islam), as an eternal entity, creative, benevolent ... Christianity and Islam can recognise each other without much difficulty. Likewise, a metaphysical approach reveals many similarities. But such an apparent convergence, underlined by the choice of qualifiers retained by the Council, cannot leave in

---

1. www.eglise.catholique.fr
2. Austin Flannery OP, general editor, *The Basic Sixteen Documents, Vatican Council II, Nostra Aetate, 3* (Dublin: Dominican Publications, 1996), p. 571.

the shade differences and even radical oppositions. The manner in which Christians and Muslims speak of God is very different.

Islam insists very strongly on the oneness of God and cannot accept the Christian revelation regarding God as Father, Son and Spirit. The concept of the Trinity is not understood. It is refused as part of a rejection of polytheism. The text of the Qur'an is generally understood by the Muslim tradition to say that Christians have altered, nay falsified the Biblical writings to make them affirm the Trinity (Qur'an, 4:171; 5:116).

Not only can there not be several persons in God, but furthermore there cannot be an incarnation. The latter, for Islam, is an attack on the transcendence of God. Indeed, Islam considers that God is very close to the human being, but also is totally different to him in nature. Muslims refuse to 'associate' any creature with God. It is therefore neither possible nor serious to affirm that a being can be true God and true man (Qur'an 3:59; 5:72; 43:59). One must indeed say that the impression which Christians are left with on reading the Qur'an is that its knowledge concerning Christianity is very poor and very often inexact.

The Qur'an doesn't accept the death of Jesus on the cross. In reality it says the crucifixion of Jesus was, for those who witnessed the scene, a deception or an illusion (certain commentators will later speak of a double who was crucified in the place of Jesus, whom God had brought into his presence). From this, there follows that no salvation comes from Christ Jesus (Qur'an 4:157-159). The latter is only a great prophet, born of the Virgin Mary, who has come to bring to mankind the Gospel, a message really coming from God but which has been deformed by Christians. Jesus is therefore simply a human being. For Islam, Jesus, being a prophet, undergoes trials as is to be expected but because he is truly a messenger of God he cannot know final failure.

Islam contains no mediation and rejects what it sees as an obstacle between God and men, while for Christianity salvation is given by Jesus Christ, the only mediator between God and men.

For Islam, as for Christianity, God speaks to men and there exist Holy Scriptures. But the understandings of revelation are very different: the Qur'an is the fruit of a dictation from God to Mohammed, it is the word of God such as God himself expresses it and utters it. Some would go so far as to say that it is eternal and uncreated. But this majority position is today subject to debate among Muslim scholars and believers. Some of them do not hesitate to speak about the interpretation of the Qur'an. For Christians, it is God who has inspired the Biblical authors who wrote the books of the Bible making use of the words and the literary forms of their time. For Muslims, the affirmations of the Qur'an have the authority of the Word of God. For this reason, dogmatic dialogue has been made very difficult regarding these essentials questions. Without ignoring these fundamental differences, it must be noted that dialogue is possible in other areas of faith such as prayer, the moral life, creation, the meaning of man …

2. It is right to go further into this question by noting carefully points in favour of a real dialogue. Vatican II has this sentence: 'But the plan of salvation also includes those who acknowledge the Creator, first among whom are the Moslems: they profess to hold the faith of Abraham, and together with us they adore the one, merciful God who will judge humanity on the last day.'[3]

This sentence of the Council employs the expression 'with us they adore', which shows a real relationship among believers

---

3. Ibid., *Lumen Gentium*, 16, pp. 21–2.

facing together towards God the Creator. The points held in common are also underlined in this quotation when it indicates a certain number of characteristics both Christians and Muslims hold in common. Our perception of the mystery of God isn't the same. For Christians, the incarnation of the Son of God has transformed things: 'No one has ever seen God. It is God the only Son, who is close to the Father's heart, who has made him known. '(Jn 1:18).

The theological dialogue concerning God develops in a climate of intimate self-revelation. It requires sympathy among the interlocutors. But at the same time it demands a real clarity about the identity of the Christian faith. That which Christ has made known to us of God is of an exceptional richness: to contemplate the Trinity and to speak about it is to show how it is the source of our spiritual life and of our manner of acting.

It is good to return to the address of St John Paul II at Casablanca to the young Muslims, on 19 August 1985. Here are a few extracts:

> I believe that we, Christians and Muslims, must recognise with joy the religious values that we have in common, and give thanks to God for them. Both of us believe in one God the only God, who is all Justice and all Mercy; we believe in the importance of prayer, of fasting, of almsgiving, of repentance and of pardon; we believe that God will be a merciful judge to us at the end of time, and we hope that after the resurrection he will be satisfied with us and we know that we will be satisfied with him.
>
> Loyalty demands also that we should recognise and respect our differences. Obviously the most fundamental is the view that we hold on the person and work of Jesus of

Nazareth. You know that, for the Christians, this Jesus causes them to enter into an intimate knowledge of the mystery of God and into a filial communion by his gifts, so that they recognise him and proclaim him Lord and Saviour.

Those are important differences, which we can accept with humility and respect, in mutual tolerance; there is a mystery there on which, I am certain, God will one day enlighten us.[4]

Finally, on his recent apostolic journey in Turkey, Pope Benedict XVI declared to those responsible for the religious affairs of the country: 'Pope Gregory VII spoke about the special charity which Christians and Muslims owe to each other since "we believe and we confess a single God, even if we do so in a different ways, each day praising him and venerating him as creator of the centuries and sovereign of this world".'[5]

✠ *Pierre-Marie Carré, President of the Doctrinal Commission of the French Bishops, 11 February 2008.*

---

4. *Documentation Catholique* 1985, p. 945.
5. Patr. Latine, 148, 451 – cf. *Documentation Catholique*, 2007, p. 12.

Acknowledgements

I would like to thank the Trappist monks of Notre-Dame de l'Atlas at Midelt in Morocco for warmly welcoming me into their community life on six occasions, starting with my first visit in 2004; Dom Luke Bell OSB who read the first draft of this book and made many useful suggestions; Br Adrien Candiard OP, for sending me the text of his play *Pierre & Mohamed*; Fr Anselme Tarpaga M. Afr. who photocopied and forwarded an important article; Abbot Éric of Aiguebelle monastery who gave me permission to translate the Testimony of Fr Christian in Appendix 1; Mgr Vincent Landel, Archbishop of Rabat, Morocco, who gave me permission to translate and publish his reflection on the Danish caricatures, in 2006, of the Prophet Mohammed, *Si l'autre devenait vraiment mon frère* in Appendix 2 and Fr Christophe Roucou of the French Episcopal Conference who did likewise for my translation of *Notes Doctrinales: Comment chrétiens et musulmans parlent-ils de Dieu?* in Appendix 3. I would also like to thank Abbot Luke and my fellow monks at Worth Abbey for supporting my interest in Christian–Muslim dialogue and the staff at Veritas for their sympathetic support in the editing and design of this book.

Some of the chapters have been previously published in *Religious Life Review* and *Doctrine and Life*, two periodicals published by the Dominicans in Dublin, and in *The Furrow*, an Irish pastoral monthly magazine. I am very grateful to their respective editors, Tom Jordan OP, Bernard Treacy OP and Fr Ronan Drury for giving me permission to incorporate these articles, in whole or in part, into this book:

'Learning to Love the Stranger', *Spirituality*, 92 (September/October 2010).

'Br Luc of Tibhirine: An Everyday Saint?', *Spirituality*, 102 (May/June 2012).

'Br Michel of Tibhirine', *Spirituality*, 107 (March/April 2013).

'The Dialogue of Friendship', *Spirituality*, 113 (March/April 2014).

'Gospel Encounters in a Muslim Land', *Doctrine and Life*, 59 (October 2009).

'Not to Convert but to Understand', *The Furrow*, 60 (July/August 2009).

'Christian–Muslim Dialogue', *The Furrow*, 62 (December 2011).